Possession

Chandler & Sharp Series in Cross-Cultural Themes

GENERAL EDITOR

Douglass R. Price-Williams
University of California, Los Angeles

CONSULTING EDITORS

L. L. Langness
Robert B. Edgerton
both University of California, Los Angeles

Possession

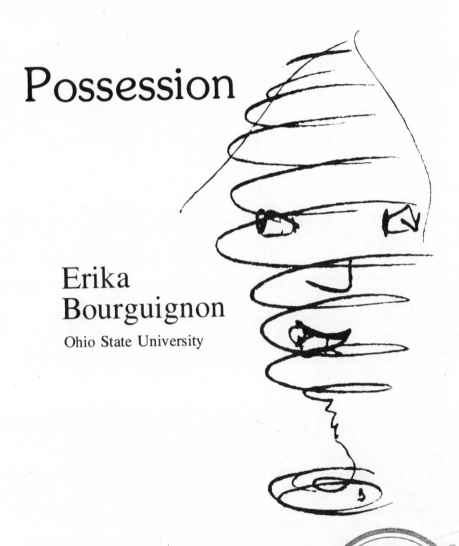

Erika
Bourguignon
Ohio State University

Chandler & Sharp Publishers, Inc.
San Francisco

Library of Congress Cataloging in Publication Data

Bourguignon, Erika,   1924-
  Possession
  (Chandler & Sharp series in cross-cultural themes)
  Filmography: p.
  Bibliography: p.
  Includes index.
    1. Spirit possession.   2. Trance.   3. Voodooism.
  I. Title
  BL482.B68   133.4'7   76-524
  ISBN 0-88316-524-4

Cover and Title Page Drawing: Paul-Henri Bourguignon
Book Design: Joseph M. Roter
Composition: Hansen & Associates Graphics

CONTENTS

Possession

1

INTRODUCTION: WHAT IS POSSESSION?

A Familiar Concept

The notion of "possession," or "spirit possession," appears to be so familiar to Americans that a definition seems hardly necessary. We find reference to it even in comic strips. Thus, Pogo's friend Albert the Alligator appears to be possessed by some "fiend" or "demon" inside his stomach. Porky thinks it should be "conjured" out of him by a witch doctor, while Pogo wonders whether it might not be "against the law to dispossess him—he prob'ly got squatter's rights."

But references to possessing spirits or demons are not limited to comic strips or swamp dwellers. Movie goers and television watchers are offered many dramas dealing with just such subjects. In one case a woman "is possessed by a strange power" so that "at night she turns into a jealous killer cougar." That is, she is "possessed" by a power which transforms her body and her spirit. In another drama, a German film, the spirit of the dead Dr. Mabuse "possesses the soul of a professor, who becomes a tool for his eccentric crimes." Here, we have transformation of behavior and of soul, but not of the body, as in the case of the unfortunate cougar woman. And in still another example, we have a variant of the Mabuse story: the "evil brain" of a dead person "invading the body of a live man." "Brain" here seems to be symbolic for soul or spirit and as a result of this possession or "invasion," again behavior is changed. The problem faced by Pogo's friend Albert the Alligator, on the other hand, appears to be physical: the fiend, monster, or demon who resides in his stomach has not changed his behavior or his consciousness.

Pogo, by Walt Kelly (4/11/73). ©1973 Walt Kelly. Courtesy Publishers-Hall Syndicate.

These four fictional examples of possession (which are presented for entertainment and require little belief) are of three types: one involves change of form as well as of consciousness and of behavior; two others involve change of consciousness and of behavior but not of form; and one involves neither change but only a physical complaint. Variously, "a strange power" causes the transformation, or the spirits or brains of dead men take hold of living bodies to continue their evil works, or a spirit entity (demon, fiend, or monster) takes hold of a body.

These uses of the subject of "possession" for purposes of entertainment suggest that this is indeed a familiar theme. The versions presented here require little explanation for the audience of these stories. The familiarity appears to be based on frequent use of the theme and this in turn is based on the existence of other spirit beliefs and possession beliefs in some segments of contemporary society. Specifically, possession belief is held to by most

---

MOVIE–Thriller
"Donovan's Brain." (1953) Lew Ayres and a good cast breathe life into
the chestnut about a dead person's evil brain invading the body of a live
man. Nancy Davis. Schratt: Gene Evans.

GHOST STORY–Drama
Doug McClure as the husband of a woman possessed by a strange
power: at night she turns into a jealous killer cougar. Jackie Cooper has a
supporting role as a rodeo clown. Winston Essex: Sebastian Cabot. (60
min.)

MOVIE–Thriller
"Dr. Mabuse vs. Scotland Yard." (German; 1964) Although Mabuse is
dead, his spirit possess the soul of a professor, who becomes a tool for
eccentric crimes. Peter van Eyck, Sabine Bethmann, Dieter Borsche. (1
hr., 45 min.)

Possession as a Theme for Entertainment. Three items from a 1972 Central Ohio
Edition of TV Guide.

contemporary churches, although in many it is only rarely called upon. The
formal role of exorcist exists in the Catholic priesthood. And all possession
beliefs of the Christian churches have a justification in the New Testament
events wherein Jesus drove out devils and healed possessed persons. Such
cases of possession were both alterations of consciousness ("madmen") and
alterations of physical state (for example: muteness, Matthew 12:22; and
crippling, Luke 13:10-13). Oesterreich (1966; originally 1931), author of a
major modern work on possession, remarks on the striking similarity between
the New Testament accounts and cases of possession reported in later times,
and he suggests that this similarity enhances the credibility of the gospels. It
should be noted also, however, that the similarity is undoubtedly in part due
to the fact that subsequent cases of possession were indeed modeled on these
earlier ones. We shall return later to take a closer look at Western ideas on
possession. For now, we may just note its familiarity, both in the field of
popular entertainment and in the field of religious belief.

There are some common themes and some differences here. Both in the
popular themes and in the religious ones mentioned so far, possession is seen
as involuntary and undesirable, harmful, and something to be rid of. And
there are two forms of possession which may be distinguished: one form of
possession causes a change in bodily functioning; the other form of possession alters consciousness, awareness, the personality or will of the individual. This latter sort we may call *possession trance* to distinguish it from the
former type. There are also some differences from the New Testament
account to be found in the popular entertainment theme: whereas the gospels

speak of possession by demons or unclean spirits, the films deal with spirits of the dead prolonging their existence in other bodies. The films, too, tie in with other themes familiar in horror tales: were-animals, mad scientists, multiple personalities of the Jekyll-Hyde variety.

In addition to the negative view of possession as involuntary and fearful there is yet another view in the Judeo-Christian tradition, one which, however, has not been particularly influential in popular culture: the view that a spirit sent by God, or the Holy Ghost, may take over some aspect of the individual's functioning. This view has found its most popular expression in American Pentecostalism and more recently in what has come to be called the charismatic revival. Its most dramatic expression is found in glossolalia or speaking in tongues, but it is also found in such other "gifts of the spirit" as the gift of interpreting tongues or the gift of prophecy. The reason that these themes have not been reflected in the popular literature, apart from descriptions of religious groups and religious leaders, is that a good deal of strong popular belief in them exists. Pentecostals and neo-Pentecostals believe that speaking in tongues reveals the action of the Holy Spirit in the person, or at least in his speech, over which the individual has only limited control. Some believe that these are actually unknown natural languages, the meaning of which is discoverable if only a speaker of the particular languages were present. Others are somewhat more cautious on this issue, but all appear to agree that speaking in tongues is a sign of what is referred to as "baptism in the spirit."

The current developments of the charismatic or neo-Pentecostal movements have attracted a good deal of attention from the news media. In 1973, a widely reported Catholic charismatic conference at Notre Dame University brought together some 20,000 people, including several bishops and a cardinal of the church. Although Pentecostalism among Protestants has existed in the United States since the turn of the century, it was traditionally a phenomenon of the uneducated and the poor, and marginal to the major denominational churches. Outward manifestations have included snake handling, strychnine drinking, dancing, rolling about on the floor, screaming, and great emotional outbursts. The current wave is being noted for its spread among the educated and the major churches. Behavior is restrained and respectable; the clergy and the structures of the churches are respected. Yet the key element of worship remains the essentially ecstatic experience.

The concept of spirit possession, then, as it appears in contemporary America ranges from entertainment and unbelief to deeply felt religious conversion and ecstasy, from fearful evil to highest good. And though some of the evil views of possession appear in the context of entertainment (such as Blatty's 1971 novel and later film, *The Exorcist*, or Ken Russell's controversial 1971 film *The Devils*), these are often based on authentic events that took place within the context of the Catholic Church, and involve present or past beliefs.

When the Western reader, schooled in Christian or popular culture themes, discovers that beliefs in spirit possession exist in other societies, he may not find this surprising at all, since he has met such beliefs in several forms in his own society. If he is one who does not share these beliefs and considers them simple and perhaps outmoded, he is likely to see in such beliefs in other societies something outmoded and superstitious as well, something he might expect from such "backward" peoples. If he is an untrained observer of the customs and beliefs of other people—and many reports in the past have come to us from such untrained observers—he may interpret what he is told and what he sees in terms of his own notions of what "backward and superstitious" people believe in. In doing so he may ascribe to these people possession beliefs, which in fact they do not hold. Such reports, and there are a great many of them, complicate our understanding of the distribution of beliefs and practices among traditional peoples and the place these beliefs and practices have in the total patterns of their societies.

Beliefs current in our own society, now or in the past, whether we share them or not, tend to block our ability to hear and see what goes on elsewhere and tend to color our understanding of what we see. Since the ability of the anthropologist to observe is his best instrument for the study of peoples of different and unfamiliar cultures, that instrument must, therefore, be guarded, if at all possible, against contamination.

Just how widespread are beliefs in possession, then? What role do they play in the lives of other peoples? How is possession manifested? Or better, what kinds of behavior or experience are identified or interpreted as possession? Who is most likely to be thought possessed, and what are the consequences of possession for a person? Is there one kind of "possession behavior" that recurs in many societies? Is possession desired or feared? How do possession behavior and possession belief relate to other aspects of society, such as religion, social organization, the status of women, beliefs in witchcraft, the use of drugs? We shall attempt to look at these and other aspects of our subject in what follows. But first, let us attempt some definitions.

Some Definitions

The Hastings *Dictionary of the Bible* tells us that *possession* is "the coercive seizing of the spirit of a man by another spirit, viewed as superhuman, with the result that the man's will is no longer free but is controlled, often against his wish, by this indwelling person or power." The article goes on to say that the possessing spirit or power may be evil or good. The central focus of this scriptural definition is on the matter of will—a person is made to act or speak without willing to do so, indeed often in direct opposition to his will. The Old Testament example of Balaam (Numbers 22-24) comes to mind, where, wishing to curse the tribes of Israel, Balaam is forced by God to bless them. Such an example shows us a split between will and performance, a split of which the actor is quite conscious. However, in addition to such psychological alterations, biblical, particularly New Testament examples, also indicate that the term *possession* may be applied to purely physical ailments or manifestations, such as lameness or deafness.

It is interesting that the split in consciousness so characteristic of certain biblical forms of possession appears also in postbiblical forms, which, however, seem to be patterned after them. Many such historically documented cases are cited by Oesterreich. That is to say, the phenomenon of split consciousness or of compulsive action against which the victim appears to be helpless appears primarily in Christian and Jewish cases of possession. In fact, in a review of the ethnographic literature on hundreds of societies, we have not encountered this phenomenon. Rather, we are more likely to find a total transformation, the apparent substitution of one personality by another.

Oesterreich (1966:17) defines *possession* as follows: "The patient's organism appears to be invaded by a new personality." Possession is manifested in a change of physiognomy and of voice and by the appearance of a strange individuality. Oesterreich furthermore differentiates between "spontaneous" (that is, involuntary) and "voluntary" (that is, induced) forms of possession.

It is clear that the types of possession Oesterreich speaks of involve psychological changes, changes in behavior and consciousness. The lameness and deafness, for example, of certain New Testament cases of possession, which appear to be entirely physical in nature, do not fit this author's categories.

It is important here to recognize that the uses of the word *possession* by the biblical authors, by the author of the dictionary article, and by Oesterreich involve two very different matters. On the one hand, these authors refer to a *belief* in possession and on the other hand, they describe certain types of *sensations* and *behavior*. The belief concerns spirits, powers, persons, "viewed as superhuman" at least in some cases, which can take over the will or consciousness of man. They can do so at their own discretion (possession is then "spontaneous") or at the call of the human being involved (possession is then "voluntary"). Where no belief exists in such spirit entities or in the ability of such entities to behave in such a way, "possession" as a concept will, of course, not exist either. Thus, *possession* is a term which refers to *belief* of a group of people under study, or, perhaps, to the belief held by a given author. On the other hand, at least some of the outward manifestations which are ascribed to "possession" in some societies may be ascribed to other causes elsewhere.

For example, the nineteenth-century French psychiatrist Jean Martin Charcot noted the similarity in the behavior of his hysterical patients with that of "possessed" persons exorcised by the clergy at earlier times. He and his students, however, interpreted the patients' conditions as due not to possession by the devil but rather as due to natural causes accessible to medical science.

Among hysterical symptoms observed, the phenomena of dissociation and of multiple personality are perhaps the most striking. In many of the medieval cases of demoniacal possession that Oesterreich reviews, for example, there seem to be fully developed personalities that appear and replace those of the victim or patient, and it is these personalities that are expelled by the exorcist. It is these too who perform various actions, such as speaking in foul and blasphemous language, of which the subject is aware but against which he or she is helpless. In modern psychiatric practice also such examples occur. Some have been reported in recent years in such books as *The Three Faces of Eve* (Thigpen and Cleckley, 1957) and *Sybil* (Schreiber, 1973). A modern psychiatrist is unlikely to explain these as due to the presence of other persons or individualities; rather, the phenomenon is explained through the patient's life history. A cure is brought about both by tracing of the sources of the personalities and also by hypnosis.

The anthropologist Horace Miner (1960:164-167) reports that among the Hausa of West Africa sleeping sickness is believed to be due to spirit possession. Again, modern medicine offers a different explanation in response to the same set of symptoms. According to Opler (1958), in North India deviant, disrespectful behavior is explained as due to spirit possession, for this is the only way in which such breach of custom can be accounted for.

The point which needs to be emphasized here is simply this: "possession" is an idea, a concept, a belief, which serves to interpret behavior. The anthropologist, who is interested in the beliefs and behaviors of human groups, can speak of "possession" only when he finds such a belief among the people he is studying. On the other hand, he is also interested in their behavior and will want to know what types of behaviors are interpreted as possession by the particular group. The Jews of the time of Jesus attributed two classes of behavior to possession by "unclean spirits." On the one hand, there were madmen; they were characterized by the states in which spirits spoke out of people—spirits who answered questions and revealed their names, and left when ordered to do so by Jesus. On the other hand, there were spirits that did not speak. The possessed persons were not thought to be insane, but rather they were deaf, or mute, or lame. And these spirits could be exorcised also. In the first instance, the possession the people believed in revealed itself in a psychological alteration; in the second, in a physical alteration. The distinction between these two types of possession is important, and appears in much of the literature, although it is usually not made explicitly. To make it explicit, we shall call the first type *possession trance*. We shall say that a belief in *possession* exists, when the people in question hold that a given person is changed in some way through the presence in or on him of a spirit entity or power, other than his own personality, soul, self, or the like. We shall say that *possession trance* exists in a given society when we find that there is such a belief in possession and that it is used to account for alterations or discontinuity in consciousness, awareness, personality, or other aspects of psychological functioning.

In psychological and psychiatric terms, what we are calling *possession trance* includes a variety of different phenomena. However, they all share alteration of consciousness, of sensory modalities, and the like. Our classification is, therefore, rather rough. It is necessary to proceed in this manner, however, for two reasons: First, many of the descriptions that are available to us are not sufficiently detailed or specific to permit going beyond this level of classification; indeed, many are so vague as not to qualify even for this level and we must omit them from consideration altogether. Second, even where rather detailed information is available, there is disagreement among trained observers whether, for example, it is appropriate to speak of "hypnosis" or whether we are dealing with "abnormal" behavior, and whether terms such as "hysterical dissociation" are appropriate.

This disagreement leads to the question of just what we might mean by "abnormal" or "pathological," a difficult subject on which only limited agreement exists. We might begin by asking: Do the people among whom possession trance occurs consider it "abnormal"? Do they say the person who experiences such a state is "crazy"? Do they say, "Something must be done about this so that he can go back to functioning like a normal person?" And just what does this "functioning" involve? The answer must be that in some societies, under some circumstances, it is considered a "bad thing" to go into possession trance and something must be done about it. In other places, going into possession trance is considered a fine and desirable thing. We shall take a closer look at these two views and some others a bit later on. But, the reader might ask, regardless of the view of the members of a particular society, what does the "objective observer" say? Isn't it possible that a highly trained and objective psychologist or psychiatrist, one who doesn't share the particular traditional beliefs, can make a judgment in psychiatric terms alone? After all, perhaps everyone in that society lives under certain delusions and misconceptions? And this question brings us then to the even more difficult problem of reaching a culture-free definition of mental health.

It is perhaps safest, in cross-cultural terms, to speak of "deviants," people whose behavior in some manner places them outside the range of normal variations of behavior within a given society. We might then have to ask: How many people in this society at one time or another manifest the symptoms of possession trance? Who are they? How is their behavior evaluated and judged by others, and how by themselves? And what is done about it?

On the first question, we have little hard information, except such statements as: "this behavior is very widespread," or, "is very widespread among women," or "among people of a given age group," say, young wives. How the behavior is evaluated and what is done about it are often closely linked. Here we can differentiate essentially three categories: (1) societies where the behavior is desired and often intentionally induced, (2) societies where the behavior is feared and vigorous efforts are made to drive out the spirit supposed to be in residence (often with physical violence) and, (3) perhaps most interesting, societies where the initial spontaneous behavior is considered deviant and perhaps sick, and where a cure involves bringing about possession trance in a controlled setting. Therapy, in this last category, does not consist in stopping the possession-trance behavior but, as it were, in domesticating it, in developing a new personality and a new status in the society. Here then, possession-trance illness and cure in fact constitute a form of religious initiation. The ability to work through a personal psychological crisis in a culturally acceptable way makes the experience one of personality growth and reorganization. A phenomenon which could have been disruptive to both the sufferer and the society is used as a social asset rather than as a liability. The rituals of therapy and the acquisition of new ritual status by the new cult member or shaman thus are methods of social adaptation.

These comments are of some importance when we consider some of the statements made and some of the terminology used in the literature. For example, Guthrie (1973:39-8), a psychologist with cross-cultural experience, speaks of "possession states" and says that they "are among the most commonly discussed behavior disorders in the anthropological literature." He then goes on to describe these states, and we find them to be what we here term "possession trance"—possession being the interpretation placed by the society's members on a trance or state of altered consciousness. He goes on to say that they are really not exotic since they occur in our own society in the context of Pentecostal ritual. And furthermore he states (p. 39-9) that "Within a religious context it [the possession state] may be considered not only normal but desirable; when it occurs in the form of fainting or functional epileptic seizures, it becomes defined as a clinical problem. . . . Seizures with loss of consciousness but without demonstrable physical pathology are a diagnostic problem for the neurologist. When confirmed as functional, they serve as another example of a possession state that has been learned, but that the subject claims not to control consciously." Here perhaps one should add that such a condition is properly referred to as a "possession state" (or possession trance) *if and only if* a belief in possession exists in the population.

If such behavior is learned in a society where such a belief is absent, then it will have another explanation and the term *possession* is not properly applied. Behavior that is learned presumably has been offered reinforcement, if we are to believe the learning theorists. But this reinforcement may well be idiosyncratic, as in the hysterical patient; in that cast it does not involve the religious framework of possession belief or other ritualized ideologies. We must then disagree with Guthrie, when he goes on to say (p. 39-9): "Societies whose members do not believe in possession by supernatural agencies *rarely* [my italics] produce a member who shows any of these behavior patterns." To the contrary, as the widespread patterns of hysteria studied by the nineteenth-century French psychiatrists would attest, the *behavior patterns* were not rare. But we cannot call them "possession states" since a belief in possession by some psychological or spiritual entity was not operative in those cases.

The difficulty arises perhaps entirely as a result of Guthrie's reference to "possession states" as "behavior patterns." Possession, as we have insisted, is a belief, a cultural belief, a shared and not idiosyncratic belief. Insofar as the behavior involves acting out a personality which is believed in, concerning which there are shared expectations, to that extent surely "possession states" cannot exist in societies where such beliefs are absent. Nevertheless, if we speak in very general terms about dissociation, fugue states, multiple personalities, fainting, functional epileptic seizures and other behavior of an apparently hysterical type, then the behavior is probably universal and occurs in all societies; however, it should not properly be referred to as "possession states."

It should be noted, furthermore, that where such states occur with a traditional religious explanation, this explanation is not necessarily one involving a concept of "possession." Particularly where hallucinations (or visions) are involved, the religious theory traditionally used is more likely to be one of a spiritual trip or voyage, the absence of the soul, and/or its adventures and encounters with various forces or beings.

In sum, we must distinguish between several large groups of explanations of altered states of consciousness: a secular type of explanation (such as drugs, fever, hysteria, schizophrenia) and two religious or supernaturalistic explanations: soul absence and possession. Only possession will concern us in what follows.

Just as we have distinguished between possession trance and possession, then, we may distinguish between possession trance and trance with other explanations. If we limit ourselves to societies with sacred or supernaturalistic explanations of altered states of consciousness, we find that both forms are very widespread indeed. In fact, among American Indian groups in particular, both in North and South America, such a state only relatively rarely occurs in the form of possession trance. In an extensive study of hundreds of societies, we found that in North America 47% and in South America 36% of the societies had no possession belief at all, yet had ritualized forms of trance.[1]

---

[1]The Cross-cultural Study of Dissociational States was supported in full by Public Health Service Research Grant MH-07463 from the National Institute of Mental Health. The study was directed by me at the Ohio State University from 1963 to 1968. A summary of the results is discussed in my "Introduction: A Framework for the Comparative Study of Altered States of Consciousness" (in Bourguignon, ed., 1973b). Further reference to this research will be made below.

Some Examples

What is and what is not possession belief and possession trance may be clarified by describing instances.

We have already mentioned various examples of possession belief from both the Old and the New Testaments. Cases patterned on this tradition are still occasionally reported. Janet (1898) presented the following case:

. . . He murmured blasphemies in a deep and solemn voice: "Cursed be God," said he, "cursed the Trinity, cursed the Virgin . . ." then in a higher voice and with eyes full of tears: "It is not my fault if my mouth says these horrible things, it is not I . . . it is not I. . . . I press my lips together so that the words may not come through, may not break forth, but it is useless; the devil then says these words inside me, I feel plainly that he says them and forces my tongue to speak in spite of me."

. . . The demon twisted his arms and legs and made him endure cruel sufferings which wrung horrible cries from the wretched man. (Janet, cited by Oesterreich, 1966:43)

A more recent example (Israel and North, 1961) came to light as a result of the death of a five-year-old boy in a small Alsatian village in 1960. The following are the results of an inquest. The mother was reported to have been an illiterate, mentally deficient person, who told the social worker the following: The boy had a spell cast on him by a person, who would bring him gifts, which contained evil spirits. Though the mother tried to get rid of these gifts, the evil spirits took possession of the boy and "made him misbehave with his parents."

At night the evil spirits tortured the boy and made him groan and scream. The mother first tried to lock him in the basement, then she fought against the spirits with holy water and by placing brooms upside down against all doors. But the evil spirits were stronger; they cracked the walls of the house, created air currents and prevented the fire from burning and even succeeded in making her prayers come out as curses and swear words. She tried to have a priest exorcise the house but could not find anyone willing to do so. Then there was only one thing left for her to do—to beat Jacques until the evil spirits left him. He would lose consciousness and when he came to he would be good and normal for some time. . . . Jacques had been killed by the evil spirits, not by the beatings she had given him; she knew that children possessed by evil spirits never lived very long.

In the first case, cited from Janet, we have a case of altered will and awareness, interpreted as possession, that we might term possession trance. In the next case, the mother's prayers that come out as curses and swear words appear to fit into the same category. However, the child's misbehavior and his groaning and screaming are rather different. Here there is a child's behavior which might be accessible to various secular explanations, interpreted by his mother as "possession" by evil spirits. There is no evidence of an altered state of consciousness.

In the medieval tradition the term *possession* is sometimes also used in a larger and somewhat misleading sense. Thus, Freud (1923) discusses a case of "demoniacal possession" found in seventeenth-century documents. Upon inspection, however, this case refers to a pact with the devil and visions (or hallucinations) of the devil, but not "possession" in the sense used here—that is, the individual does not acquire another personality thought to be that of the devil, a strange voice does not issue from him, nor is there similar behavior. He is himself, except that he has made an agreement to allow the devil to have his soul in exchange for worldly goods.

Some types of behavior are not clearly to be classed as possession trance merely on the basis of observation. In each case, it is necessary to have the native explanation. This applies very clearly to such behavior as firewalking and speaking in tongues (glossolalia). For example: the German psychiatrist Pfeiffer (1971:121-122) reports on his observations of a Chinese firewalking ceremony in Java. In the course of the ceremony, several men ran across a specially prepared bed of glowing charcoal, struck their chests with cloths dipped in boiling oil and boiling sugar and cut their tongues with a sword. Three of the men carried out these actions in a trance state, their faces rigidly expressionless. However, it appears that the accompanying belief system does not involve possession. Rather, the men believe themselves to be transformed into fire spirits and, therefore, to be immune to the dangers of fire. A fourth man had a different cultural background: he was a Christian, from the island of Amboina. He did not appear to go into an altered state, and appears to have been quite conscious of his actions throughout. He explained to the author that protection against the fire is achieved through mystical force which is acquired through ascetic and pure living and particularly through faith in divine protection.

In modern Greece and Bulgaria, firewalking is also practiced. In Greece, it appears that firewalkers, who practice their ritual in honor of St. Constantine, are believed to be possessed by that saint (Michael-Dede 1973).[2] In Bulgaria, to the contrary, firewalking appears to be linked to a hallucinatory state (Schipkowensky, 1963). It should be noted that firewalking presents a problem of skill and of mastery over fear of fire, but does not require an altered state to be accomplished unscathed. The important point to stress here is that what appears to be identical behavior may be accompanied by quite different cultural interpretations as well as by different subjective states. Furthermore, the subjective states are directly influenced and conditioned by the cultural explanations.

The same comment applies to the trance behavior termed glossolalia or speaking in tongues.[3] Here, too, the behavior involves certain basic sim-

---

[2]The documentary film, *The Astenaria*, by P. C. Haramis and K. Kakouri, shows the firewalking ceremony in a Greek village.

[3]For an excellent discussion of the phenomenon of glossolalia and its development in a particular Mexican Apostolic church, see F. D. Goodman (1972).

ilarities and some local elaborations, and is subject to a variety of interpretations, among them: possession by the Holy Ghost, which produces the vocalizations; a special form of prayer which is a gift of the Holy Ghost; speech in actual languages unknown to the speaker and produced as a supernatural gift.

One more type of belief should be mentioned here, since it is sometimes discussed in the context of "possession," and that is belief in reincarnation. Ian Stevenson,[4] a psychiatrist interested in what he calls "cases suggestive of reincarnation" notes certain similarities between the two and states:

> The difference between reincarnation and possession lies in the extent of displacement of the primary personality achieved by the influence of the "entering" personality. Possession implies either a partial influence with the primary personality continuing to retain some control of the physical body, or a temporary (if apparently complete) control of the physical organism with later return of the original personality. (Stevenson 1966:340)

He then goes on to list six different types of possession ranging from partial temporary possession to complete permanent possession beginning at conception. Thus, at the last point, possession and reincarnation become fully synonymous. (However, since there is no personality to displace at all in the latter case, it is difficult to see how this can be counted as possession.) In the book in question, Stevenson presents cases from India, Ceylon, Brazil, the Tlingit Indians of Alaska, and from Lebanon. The question is not raised whether the people he interviewed consider that the presumed reincarnation is, indeed, an example of possession. And in several of these societies, as in Brazil and Ceylon, an active possession-trance cult exists. Stevenson discusses, in fact, his own concepts of possession and reincarnation, *not* those of the people he is studying. This distinction is of some importance.

For example, among various Eskimo groups, it has been reported repeatedly, the shaman is believed to be possessed by protective spirits or animal spirits, that enter his body and speak through his mouth. Balikci (1970) reports this for the Netsilik Eskimo, and Lantis (1950) generalizes this for the Eskimo groups of Alaska. It is also true that there was a widespread belief in reincarnation among the Eskimo, who believed that human beings had two kinds of souls; a breath soul and a name soul. It was the name soul, carrying with it the personality of its previous host, which was believed to be reincarnated in a child before birth. A pregnant woman would call out several names and one of these would enter the unborn child, facilitating the delivery (Balikci, 1970). From the point of view of the present discussion, what matters is that the possession trance experienced by the shaman and the reincarnation of the name soul seem to be totally unrelated in the Eskimo

---

[4]I am indebted to Dr. Lynn Ager for drawing my attention to the writings of Stevenson, and to some of the Eskimo materials discussed.

view. In the first place, there is possession trance; in the second, there is not. The shaman is possessed by animal spirits and other nonhuman spirits, who have their existence independent of the shaman; in reincarnation, the name souls are those of deceased human beings, which exist as nonembodied entities only between incarnations. All the evidence suggests that the Eskimo do not perceive a relation between these two ideas, as Stevenson would have it.

The Approach of this Inquiry

The anthropologist, it must be remembered, studies the beliefs and practices of various human societies. As such, the anthropologist studies the views people have on spirits and spirit possession, on reincarnation and other matters, and it is in this light that he considers the evidence which people adduce concerning their experiences with spirits, powers, etc. This "evidence" sheds light on the way in which a given human group perceives the universe and how this perception can account for human behavior. The anthropologist's task is not to learn about spirits, possession, reincarnation and such matters as ends in themselves. He is interested in spirit beliefs *only* as they can inform us about people. This difference between the anthropologist and others such as the parapsychologist and the religionist is of crucial importance. In the following pages, therefore, we shall consider a variety of phenomena related to spirit-possession belief. Here we shall speak of possession and possession trance *if and only if* such beliefs exist in the societies under discussion, and *as, and only as*, these beliefs function in the particular societies. We shall not attempt, in other words, to impose definitions of our own.

The different beliefs and behaviors of human societies are the subject matter of our investigation. Knowledge of the beliefs helps us to understand behavior, for without such knowledge, behavior is incomprehensible. Such an investigation does not require us to share a belief in spirits or in spirit possession. In studying the beliefs of others and in respecting them, we need not make them our own. Our questions concerning the existence of a possession trance complex of belief and behavior, which exists in some societies and not in others, are not questions about the existence of spirits, but about the behavior of people, their beliefs, and their ways of life. We do not say: why do the spirits possess people in this manner in society X? Rather, we ask: why do people in society X behave in this manner and hold such beliefs? We shall deal with the case of Haiti in this fashion. As to the existence of spirits, it behooves us to maintain an attitude of healthy skepticism. The observations cited in this book are all open to quite different explanations.

2

POSSESSION BELIEF AND POSSESSION TRANCE IN HAITIAN FOLK RELIGION: A CASE STUDY

Vodou

In the Haitian folk religion of *vodou* (often called "voodoo" in the United States), possession trance is a central feature of most rituals. It has attracted a good deal of attention both in popular literature and in anthropological writings. To a Catholic missionary such as the Belgian priest J. Verschueren (1948), vodou was paganism and he was not certain that the participation of the devil might not be seen in its activities. More recent writings by members of the Catholic clergy, such as M. Laguerre (1970), take a different, more ecumenical view and seek to find the "part of truth" in this traditional system of belief and ritual.

As it exists today, vodou is a syncretic religion; that is, it contains elements originating from many historical sources.[1] In part as a result of this, vodou appears in two different lights to nonanthropologists. To some, it is an ignorant mixture of poorly understood traditions of various sources, the whole being a superstitious hodgepodge. To others, it appears as a repository of exotic and esoteric mysteries. To the anthropologist, it is neither. Rather, he sees it as the beliefs that guide the actions of a people, and if the actions are to be understood and not to be seen merely as erratic and arbitrary, then the world view which presides over this behavior must be understood.

---

[1]Among the many works on Haiti and Haitian religion, the following should be cited: Herskovits (1973b), Deren (1953), Métraux (1959), Courlander (1960).

16

When African slaves were brought to the French colony of St. Domingue in the eighteenth century, they carried with them the beliefs and traditions of their tribes. They were converted, at least superficially, to Catholicism. From this combination resulted beliefs and practices that included elements of several African cultures and some elements of Catholicism. The word *vodou* itself is derived from the Dahomean term *vodun* for spirit. The spirits are classed into "nations"—a term which has no political meaning in this context. The names of these nations, however, are virtually a list of African tribal names; witness Nago (referring to certain Yoruba-speaking groups of the Dahomean-Nigerian border area), Rada (derived apparently from Allada, the name of a Dahomean town), Ibo (another Nigerian tribe), Congo. The spirits also have names of Catholic saints (Herskovits, 1937a), and pictures of Catholic saints are shown as representing Afro-Haitian spirits. At the same time, these spirits are also represented during rituals by ground drawings made with white flour, corn meal, coffee, ashes, and similar materials. The participants themselves, on the whole, are unaware of the multiple sources of their beliefs and practices.

The Environment of Belief

To understand the possession-trance behavior, we need to consider first the fundamental world view of vodou practitioners, who represent the vast majority of the Haitian people. They believe in God, called by the French words *Bon Dieu*; in a series of spirits called variously saints, *zanj* (from the French word for angels), *mystè* (from the French for mysteries), and *loa*. It is this last word, which has no Christian connotations and the origin of which is obscure, that shall be used here. Furthermore, there are the dead, some of whom have become transformed into loa, as well as a particular category of family dead, the twins. While a veneration of the dead has both a Christian and an African background, the cult of the twins, called by the African term *marassa*, has no European counterpart.

The cult of the spirits (the loa, the dead, and the twins) is handed down in families and is carried out by ritual experts or priests, called *houngan* (male) and *mambo* (female). A person joins a society or cult group under the direction of such a leader either because of family traditions or because of events in his or her life which have been interpreted by such a leader as a call from the spirits. Such an event might be a spontaneous possession trance, an illness or misfortune, a series of dreams, or other events deemed significant.

Many first possession experiences occur in adolescence as loss of consciousness and other forms of disordered behavior. They may occur during ceremonies in response to certain drum rhythms, during children's games, when youngsters enjoy imitating the behavior of adults and of spirits during ceremonies, or in situations of stress. If the behavior is interpreted by the person's relatives as perhaps spirit possession, a priest or priestess will be consulted, who may concur in this diagnosis, identify the spirit, and require a brief, preliminary initiation ritual. In the local view, this is done to please the spirit. The spirit will most likely be identified as one known in the family or in the cult house of the priest consulted. The subject is informed that he or she is the "horse" of a certain spirit, one who is most likely already known to the individual from attendance at rituals, from observation of experiences of others with this spirit, and from stories about such experiences. This knowledge, and the initial rituals, in effect teach the individual the appropriate behavior to be engaged in when the spirit comes, and, most importantly, the songs and drum rhythms in response to which the spirit will appear. That is to say, the novice learns the cues which will induce possession trance at appropriate ceremonies.

A number of things are implied concerning spirits in the previous paragraphs: children are taken to ceremonies in participating families from the earliest days of their lives; they hear stories about spirits as they hear anecdotes about people in their families and neighborhoods. They see dancing and hear songs and music associated with the spirits, so that by the time they experience an altered state they have learned the basic information relevant for appropriate behavior.

What remains to be learned are the cues that will initiate the altered state and an explicit identification with a given spirit entity, as well as the situations in which the cues are not to be operative. The Haitians say that a "new" spirit, one that has not previously "danced in the head" of a given person—or "mounted" a particular "horse"—is "bossal" or wild, and in order to be tamed such a spirit must be baptized. Furthermore, a bossal spirit has not yet learned to dance properly; as he is tamed, he acquires his dancing skill.

Now, there are a great many spirits and an individual in the course of time is likely to be possessed by several. One spirit, however, is the "master of his head" and it is for this particular spirit that the individual undergoes an initiation rite. Possession trance occurs properly at ceremonies of the family or ritual group to which the individual belongs. If as a guest he attends a ceremony conducted by another group, his spirits are not to appear. For any to appear is considered bad manners—on the part of the spirit—a sort of party crashing. Spirits may also appear spontaneously, that is, possession trance may occur, without the ritual setting, in response to stress situations. People whose spirits appear erratically are considered to be deranged and in need of treatment by a vodou specialist: clearly, something is wrong in the relation between human and spirit. This is a two-way relationship, in which the human "horse" is expected to gain increasing knowledge and with this, increasing control over the appearances of the spirits. In fact, elderly people are rarely possessed, because, it is said, they have gained much knowledge and because the spirits are considerate in not imposing the fatigue of a possession trance, with its dancing and sometimes acrobatics, on the elderly.

As noted, a great many spirits are believed to exist. Some important loa are known to all. Most of these have names and some characteristics that allow us to trace them back to West Africa and the Congo region; many of these spirits are also known in such other Afro-American areas as Cuba, Trinidad, and Brazil. Among these are: Ogou, the Yoruba (Nago) spirit of warfare and of iron; Damballah, the Dahomean snake spirit; and Legba, the Dahomean trickster spirit. The spirits which are venerated and invited in particular families and cult groups vary, however, so that a catalog of Haitian spirits, which has never been attempted, would run into the hundreds.[2] In this respect, it is important that some ancestors can become loa and also that new loa appear and demand to be attended to. These new loa often enough seem to relate to some aspects of the individual's personal history.

There are several differences between the Haitian cults on the one hand and, on the other, the traditional West African cults, together with the more conservative Brazilian cults such as those of San Salvador, in the state of Bahia. As has been mentioned, in Haiti an individual is likely to be possessed by several spirits, often in succession at the same ceremony, acting out a variety of roles. In the others, a person is initiated for one spirit and only this spirit is thought to be present in possession trance. This feature of the Haitian system is most significant; essentially, the system is an open one. That is, neither the number nor the character of the spirits is fixed, so that much innovation in ritual and personal expression is possible. Haitians believe that there is a similarity in character between a person and his or her spirits and also that the spirits sometimes act in ways quite opposed to the typical behavior of their human horses. The innovative aspects mean that ritual is never quite the same if we compare two families, two cult groups, two regions; there exists a good deal of individuation. Ritual is not precise and stereotyped. Often it is the spirits themselves, or rather the possession trancer, who announce ritual requirements and express wishes or dissatisfactions. On the other hand, there may be a good deal of continuity in the behavior of a given individual possessed by the same spirit, on different occasions.

A Possession-Trance Ritual Reported

Some of what has been said here can be illustrated in the description, taken from my field notes, of a vodou ceremony which I observed. It took place on Christmas Eve in the cult center and homestead of a rural houngan, in the sugar-growing area not far from Port-au-Prince.

On December 24, about six in the evening, things were in a state of preparation in the courtyard of Victor, a houngan. A few people were sitting

---

[2]See Courlander (1960), Appendix I, for lists and detailed discussions of the principal spirits and groups of spirits.

around under the open shelter. Several men were drumming, and the houngan's wife, Mme. Victor, was roasting coffee in great quantities. Two storm lamps were lit and hung in the rafters. One individual was already in possession trance, saying he was "Simbi en dé zeaux, gros neg, gros mystè." That is, the name of the spirit was Simbi of the two waters and he announced that he was an important man, an important spirit. He was also quite drunk; he is known as a drunkard, the explanation being that he had misserved his loa and that, therefore, they punish him by obscuring his mind instead of enlightening him.

Meanwhile more and more people arrived, and the Petro drums started out more determinedly, also several gourd rattles and the ogan, a resonant iron percussion instrument. Singing and a bit of dancing started. Meanwhile, preparations continued. Rather quietly a large fire was lit in the yard, the assistants of the houngan brought out a large mortar (waist high, about three feet) and two pestles, about eight feet in height. They brought in cloths and, in wrapped bundles, the leaves to be crushed to powder. When all was in order, the drums, the singing, and the dancing stopped, and Victor, with chalk, drew a design inside the mortar, to the light of a taper, and crosses on the two pestles and the hands of the men who were to do the stamping. When he had finished, the mortar, the leaves, and the pestles were covered with a sheet, the houngan and his assistants squatting on the floor beside it, removing their hats. Victor then said the Catholic prayers (three Paternoster, three Ave Maria alternating, and a credo) and then the Petro prayer, during both of which the assistants chanted responses. During the prayer one man went into possession trance. At first I could not see him from where I was sitting, but only heard his inarticulate screams and howls in the pauses between Victor's reciting and the responses of the group. When the prayer was almost finished he came forward, completely stiff-limbed, with dilated pupils and a rigid facial mask. He saluted first the drums and then various of the bystanders. He too was said to be possessed by Simbi en dé zeaux.

Then the drums started off again. (At one point before the end of the Petro prayer, several individuals called on the drums, but Victor corrected them, saying that the drummers had been right, that they were not to start until later). People began to dance, this time two or three couples facing each other. While some of them danced with considerable improvisations and changes, Monpoint, Victor's younger brother, danced it rigidly, orderly, and in form almost like a minuet. During the dancing his movements became more and more rigid, but he did not go into possession trance. He was supposed to become possessed by Malulu, who was later to lead the loa to the fire, but he did not want to get possessed and was fighting against it.

Meanwhile the two men with the pestles began to stamp the leaves. They were working at an alternating rhythm, with machinelike precision, adding their beat to that of the drums and the other instruments; gradually, and increasingly, possession trances began to occur. One woman, Augusta, a cult member who lives in Port-au-Prince, was possessed by Maît' GrandBois, the master of the forest and of the leaves. She is a woman in her thirties, tall and enormous in bulk. While in possession trance she was agitated violently, and she, or rather the possessing spirit, insisted on climbing on top of the mortar. As she stood on it, the men were obliged to go on stamping the leaves between her legs.

Then Victor's niece Josilia, who is also rather stout, was possessed, also by GrandBois. She too wanted to climb on the mortar, and a scuffle ensued between the two possessed women. Then Josilia's sister Antoinette was also possessed by the same spirit and, seeing the others, wanted to get on the mortar too, in the process of which her dress got torn. Her mother, who was watching the scene, rushed to her rescue, pinning the dress so as to keep her clothed. The end result of the struggle was that the first GrandBois, Augusta, lay down on the floor, demanding that the mortar be put on her belly, and the stamping be continued there. Then it was placed on her thighs and eventually between her thighs; meanwhile the stamping went on, at one moment with Josilia on top of the mortar and Augusta under it. She was twisting and throwing herself about as the men worked and, while the mortar was on top of her, the rhythmical stamping literally seemed to penetrate her.[3]

Meanwhile other possessions continued to arrive, in addition to Augusta, Josilia, Antoinette, and the two men possessed by Simbi en dé zeaux. Several women seemed to fall, losing their balance, one rolling on the ground. So many things were going on simultaneously, still centering about the mortar and the effort to hold it upright and go on working while the possessed women insisted on climbing on it or under it, that it was not possible to get the names of the various loa. They were not all saluted by the drums, not even recognized. The aroma of the stamped leaves became intoxicating and tremendously strong; the light of the two storm lamps grew dimmer and dimmer. At that moment about 100 to 150 people were tightly packed under the shelter, around the mortar and the drums, and strictly speaking there was no room to dance.

Outside about the fire a large crowd had gathered, mainly younger people and children and a few women with trays filled with cold drinks and edibles of various sorts which they were offering for sale. Several loa came out, skirting the fire, jumping across, disappeared again, to the cheering of the crowd. Inside, the lights had almost gone out, the drums and the stamping continued, as well as new possessions. Victor's brother Sino, a little man usually humble and deferential, was possessed by Papa Loko. He now acted like a royalty,

---

[3]Josilia had been taken rather violently, and the next day I was told that she had not wanted to be possessed by GrandBois and had tried to tie him. GrandBois in Augusta's head had told her if she would do that once more, he—GrandBois— would kill her.

full of dignity and ceremony. After several hours of pounding leaves and continuous possessions, the crowd gradually drifted outside. Several women possessed by Guédé came out—almost crawling—skirting the flames, not daring to approach. A man with a whip circled the group, beating the air, presumably to chase away evil spirits. A fight ensued among a group of young men and the whole crowd participated, though the matter was liquidated in a few minutes.

Finally the drums moved out, and then Augusta, Josilia, and a group of other women, now dressed in blue jeans, caps on their heads, their jaws tied as for corpses, cotton in their mouths and nostrils, uttering unearthly groans. They were possessed by Maît' Cimtiè, the master of the cemetery. As soon as the drums started, they began to dance, to cross the fire, but actually although it must have been rather hot, without any real violence or any real danger of burning. Antoinette and various others said to be possessed by Guédé kept a respectful distance from the fire. Then others began to dance and the dancing and singing continued the entire night. Some of the possessions changed so that in the course of the night Josilia was possessed, aside from GrandBois and Maît' Cimtiè, by Damballah and, at nine, the next morning, still by Guédé. Quite a few of the possessions hung over to the next day, although the loa are to depart at sunrise. Several walked half an hour's distance the following morning, either to their own homes or to pay visits, remaining, at least in cultural terms, still possessed.

The Possession-Trance Ritual Examined

To understand what was going on here, we must attempt to disregard the local color, the unfamiliar atmosphere, and perhaps some of the dramatic aspects of this scene.[4]

Several levels of events are involved. One level concerns the formal content of the ritual, its "program" as it were. Here we have a ritual which is part of the annual cycle, and as such expresses syncretism with Christianity; the event always occurs on Christmas Eve and some of the participants come to it after having attended midnight mass in a Catholic Church. In the ritual itself, we have the Catholic prayers which start off the proceedings, and are followed by the non-Catholic ritual. There are drawings of crosses, and the use of a bell during the prayers. These, however, are the extent of the Catholic contribution. Beyond formal content, we find that this annual ritual

---

[4]A Christmas ceremony among this same group is described by Métraux (1959). It is interesting to note that, from one year to the next, certain features remain constant, even features that to the one-time observer seem marginal to the ceremony and arising out of perhaps momentary feelings among certain individuals. As always, a single observation cannot give us a sufficient picture to assess events. It is in part for this very reason, and because of the availability of Métraux's description, that this particular ceremony has been selected for analysis here.

(which is not unique to this particular group in its major outlines) is addressed to a group of spirits, known collectively as Petro. They appear to be of Haitian origin, although some of the names are African. The Simbi group of spirits, for example, is of African origin, but they often appear together with Petro spirits. In any event, the principal ritual activity concerns medicinal leaves and the spirit who presides over them, called Maît' GrandBois. This is the first portion of the ritual, and it is followed by one centering about the spirits of the cemetery and of death, the Guédés. The leaves are to be used in curing and protective rituals throughout the year, in part as baths and in part tied up in doll-shaped bundles (*paquets*), used as powerful ritual objects. This juxtaposition between curing and death is striking, for the spirits of death are also powerful magicians. Their permission is needed to cause magical death and, as they preside over death, they also preside over cures and, even more importantly, over fertility and childbirth. The sexually suggestive nature of some of their dancing, under these circumstances, seems not particularly surprising. The presence of the Simbis is also relevant here, for, as water spirits, they are part of the death cult. Spirits of the dead are believed to spend several years under the waters, until the family has a ritual performed which speeds them on to the next stage of their posthumous existence. Simbi is a powerful magician and the paquets are made under his auspices as well as those of Maît' GrandBois.

Another level of events concerns the social groups involved. There are members of a family who assemble at this time, some having come considerable distances to be present. There are members of a cult group, assembling under their leader; the memberships of cult group and of the family overlap somewhat. There is interaction between people as their "normal" selves and interaction among persons in altered states of consciousness, that is, supposedly, interaction among spirits; and, in addition, there are interactions between spirits and humans. Furthermore, a given person, such as Josilia, for example, acts and reacts as a number of different personalities in the course of this period of a dozen or so hours.

The interactions among personalities might be considered a bit more closely. For example, the houngan Victor is not in possession trance at any time during the ceremony and although he is not dramatically active, as are some of the other participants, he is in complete control of events. Two of his brothers, however, who, in everyday life are minor figures in the organization of the family and the cult group, play important roles in the Christmas ritual. Indeed, without their cooperation, the rituals could not proceed. It is, therefore, interesting that one of them, Monpoint, attempts unsuccessfully to restrain his spirit from coming. The other, Sino, who is treated with little respect by members of his family, plays the role of a very powerful spirit and appears to gain much satisfaction from this. Indeed, his spirit lingered on longer than others the following morning, and was given much respect and deference by the man's wife and daughters, who are usually quite oblivious of him. These two examples suggest that for people whose self-respect is in need of bolstering, the possession-trance role playing, the impersonation of powerful spirits, acts as a mechanism of compensation, of balancing the neglect they experience in everyday life. It also appears to give them some real power over more dominant members of their groups. From a psychological point of view, we may consider the spirits to be alternate roles played by human beings, at appropriate occasions.

The idea that human beings may resist possession by spirits appears in the case of one of these men as well as in that of one of the women. It is considered to be a dangerous thing to try, and when possession trance occurs in spite of such efforts, it appears to be more violent and exhausting than under other circumstances. This makes good psychological sense: going into possession trance means that one "lets go" and submits to the cues of the drums and the suggestion of the setting and of one's own expectations. Resisting means that an opposite pull exists so that there is conflict and ambivalence in the individual; if this conflict is resolved by overcoming the resistance, the result may well be stressful.

It is, of course, of interest to observe the personal psychological aspect of possession-trance behavior. Yet we must keep in mind that this is only one level of meaning of this behavior. To the participants, the spirits are real, powerful entities, who overcome human individuals, ride them, engaging in vigorous and unusual behavior. That personal conflicts are ventilated in this process, that individuals may obtain satisfactions and compensations is not perceived or articulated in these terms by them. This type of discussion is alien to their view of the universe. Yet both the ritual level and the personal level exist, and the personal level gives this ritual behavior its strong emotional support. People are, quite literally, involved with all their being in their religious activities.

Another example of what is being said here is found in the case of the three women possessed by Maît' GrandBois.[5] This spirit's presence empowers the magical and medicinal force of the leaves. The physical contact between the possession trancers and the leaves, or the mortar, is, therefore, of ritual importance. A very similar scene is described by Métraux (1959) for another Christmas Eve in this group. Yet, although the sexual aspect of this activity is quite transparent to the observer, it is unrelated to the ritual meaning of the scene. It is important to note here that the actors were women and the sexual aspects of the scene relate to that fact, yet the spirits are male spirits. The

---

[5] A ceremony for Maît' GrandBois, described by Courlander (1960) for another part of Haiti, bears no resemblance to this Christmas ritual.

scene among the women, on a human and familial level, expresses strong rivalry between two sisters, in which the younger one is in a dominant position and the older, humiliated, is driven off, with her dress torn. The rivalry exists in daily life and the possession-trance behavior reinforces the real-life situation. Yet even in such a struggle, the possession trancer has the secure knowledge that things will not go too far: the torn dress is quickly fixed by an observant member who is in full normal consciousness. Possession trance is followed by amnesia; the following day Antoinette had to be told how her dress had become torn. Yet this was not a single-time event: Métraux tells us of its occurrence on another Christmas Eve!

It would appear then that, just as there is continuity in human behavior, there is also continuity in the personalities of the spirits—both as they occur in the same person on successive occasions and as they occur in different persons. Thus, learning and expectations play important parts in these role-playing activities.

Summary

To sum up, then: In Haiti, in the folk religion of vodou, we find possession trance a part of the ritual behavior. It is believed that the spirits, the loa, choose the people they possess. These are referred to as the "horses" of the spirits, who are said to "mount" them during ceremonies. Although individuals may at times attempt to avoid possession trance, it is considered desirable to be chosen by the spirits. The spirits are invited to rituals offered in their honor; specific spirits are called—and greeted—by special drum rhythms, songs and dances, and food is offered to them. They are asked to help in curing, in magic, in giving advice. It is believed that they are powerful allies, who must be respected and who must be made offerings and given the kind of homage they demand.

Nontrance Possession

Before we move on to a more analytical level of discussion of the phenomenon of possession trance, we need to note another type of Haitian belief: possession by the dead, causing illness. This kind of possession does not involve an altered state of consciousness. Rather, it is believed that certain types of sorcerers can cause illness by sending spirits of dead individuals into a victim. This type of sorcery is called "expéditions de morts." A vodou priest diagnoses an illness as being caused in such a manner and with the help of his or her spirits, attempts a cure by identifying the sorcerer and dislodging the spirits. While a concept of possession is involved here too, it is clear that we are dealing with a phenomenon of quite a different sort from the possession trance described in the preceding pages.

Two Ritual Ground Drawings: Vévé

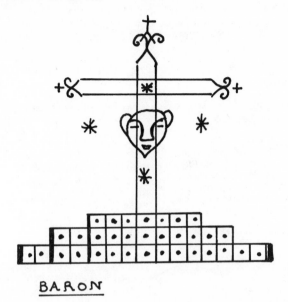

BARON

Vévé for Baron (or Baron Samedi) symbolized by a cemetery cross.

CYMBI

Vévé for Simbi (or Cymbi). The drawing suggests his relation to the cross-roads,
hence with magic.

Oraison a

RadegOnde

ORAISON
St Radegonde

Le jour du Brave est le lundi et le samedi vous irez au cimetière allumer des bogies et dire votre prière en terminant ainsi Brave je remettre ma personne en vos mains puis toute est dit

ORAISON

Radegonde brave baron samaedi gardien du cimetière grnd saint vous avez eu les peuvoirdetravcaser le purgatei ro eremn se.

Je crois o mon Sauveur que vos êtes véritablement ressussité commu vous l'avez annoncé. En trois jours avez rétabli le temple de vos temple de vos temples de vos ennemis vaiaent osé détruire Vous avez donnés votre vie et l'avez reprise quand vous avez voulu.

O Christ O fils du Dieu vivant qui est pour nous la résurrection de la vie. Je crois d'une foi ferme que la résussitera un jour.

Prayer to St. Radegonde. Sold in the market place, to be worn as a talisman; Brave, one of the Guédé group of loa, is here identified with Baron Samedi, the guardian spirit of the cemetery, and with St. Radegonde. [Translation below.]

PRAYER
St. Radegonde

The day of Brave is Monday and Saturday you will go to the cemetery to light candles and say your prayer ending thus Brave I place myself in your hands then all is said

ORISON

Radegonde Brave Baron Samedi guardian of the cemetery great saint you have had the power to prevail against [?] purgatory [?].

I believe O my Savior that you have truly risen as you had announced it. In three days have rebuilt the temple of your temples [?] that [?] your enemies had dared destroy. You have given your life and have taken it back when you wanted to.

O Christ O son of the living God who is for us the resurrection of life. I believe with firm faith that I [?] shall revive from the dead one day.

This belief in possession, unconnected to altered states of consciousness or to vodou ritual as such, serves to explain some kinds of illness that do not respond to ordinary treatments. It is connected to a complex of sorcery, or witchcraft, beliefs. The possessing spirits, several of whom may be inside a person at one time, are spirits of the dead who have been dispatched by a sorcerer to cause harm. In contrast to possession trance which is invited and desired, possession by the dead is feared and must be terminated by exorcism if the patient is not to die.

3

HAITI: SOME EXPLANATIONS

How can we understand Haitian possession belief and Haitian possession-trance behavior, which appear so strange to us? Indeed, how understand possession-trance behavior in general? Explanations abound, and, for some reason, Haitian vodou has been the focus of much of the discussion. If we do consider only the Haitian case in our attempts at explanation, we may, however, be attacking the problem at the wrong end, since it somehow assumes, if only implicitly, that we are dealing with a rare or extraordinary situation. The Haitian physician and historian J. C. Dorsainvil (1931) took the position that possession trance in his country was due to "living on nerves," even to inherited racial psychosis. As M. J. Herskovits (1937b) has pointed out, possession trance is not unique to Haiti. Possession trance and religions related to vodou are widespread among the African peoples from whom the Haitians derive, as well as among many Afro-American peoples, as in Cuba, Trinidad, and Brazil.

The Background

We know that the ancestors of the modern Haitians and of the other Afro-Americans came from West and Central Africa for the most part, and we know that they brought the basic features of their religions, specifically possession trance, with them. It would be too simple, however, to explain this phenomenon in modern Haiti entirely as a heritage of the Haitian African past. It is certainly such a heritage, but it is more. African religions survived in the Americas in various degrees of transformation. To understand these changes and the resulting modern forms, we must know both what the Africans found in the New World and also what the contemporary societies are like in which these religions flourish. Here we find great and striking

28

differences. In the Catholic areas (including Cuba and Brazil, as well as Haiti), where Afro-Catholic religions have developed, saints are identified with African-derived spirits, and we find highly individuated types of possession trance. In Protestant areas such cults do not exist (see Bourguignon, 1967). Yet enthusiastic churches of the revivalistic and Pentecostal type have flourished and are flourishing. People go into altered states of consciousness, speak in tongues, and engage in a variety of other charismatic activities. Some authors, most particularly Herskovits (1941) have argued that this behavior is to be understood as a reinterpretation of the old African possession-trance behavior. Certainly much appears in these two traditions that is similar, and at least one author, D. M. Beckman (1974), is now arguing that the characteristic American revivalistic church owes much to African influence, even among whites.

As far as Haiti is concerned, in any event, it is important to note that the Africans met a Catholic pattern of institutional religion and a type of colonial society within which their traditions could survive with two elements of transformation: For one, there was some fusion and some elimination of certain African traditions and the domination of the pattern by Dahomean and Yoruba beliefs and rites. For the other, there was a certain syncretism with some features of Catholicism. In time, native Haitian elements of belief also developed for which there are no clear African correspondences, as in the case of the Petro spirits. Haitian peculiarities of ritual grew up in a long period of separation and isolation from African sources, which began, essentially, with the end of slavery as a result of the French Revolution in 1789 and with independence in 1804. Concurrently, Haiti also broke with Rome for the major portion of the nineteenth century, hence an indigenous mixture could develop which differentiates Haitian vodou not only from its African antecedents but also from its Afro-American counterparts.

Vodou, whatever its sources and parallels, is a present-day Haitian religion that derives its vitality from its adaptation to the realities of contemporary Haitian society and culture. The elements of which it is made up can be traced in large measure to various historical sources. It has played an important role in Haiti's history, by contributing to slave revolts and to the revolution that brought about independence in 1804. Yet these sources and this historical role are not enough by themselves to explain its present-day form and, indeed, its existence. As A. Métraux (1959:365) says with some emphasis:

It is too often forgotten that Voodoo, for all its African heritage, belongs to the modern world and is part of our own civilization. . . . For a true picture, it is essential to remember that although the religion of the black peasant is still, to a large extent, African, the institutions of Haiti, its political ideals, its notion of progress, are those of a Western state. Voodoo gods, in spite of their African names and lore, are under the influence of their environment . . . the *loa* have the tastes of modern man, his morality and his ambitions. They are no longer the gods of an African tribe, exotic and remote, but deities who act and think in the industrialized world of today.

And he concludes: "Voodoo is a paganism of the West."

If only the historical sources mattered, why is there no vodou in Chicago or in Columbus, Ohio?[1] After all, the blacks of all parts of the New World stem from generally the same ancestral African regions.

The problem concerning Haitian possession belief unconnected to trance states seems to be somewhat different. As has been mentioned, Haitians believe that sorcerers, evil houngans, can send spirits of the dead against a person to cause illness by possessing him. There seems to be no clear African antecedent or parallel for this, and the European case is at best somewhat dubious. That is to say, in the European tradition a witch could cause a person to be possessed. The prime symptoms of such possession, however, were spectacular hysterical attacks, blasphemy and obscenity pronounced against the victim's will, rather than illness as in Haiti. The possessing spirits were demons (in Europe) or the spirit of the witch (in New England); in Haiti, they are anonymous dead people. These differences are important, yet a pattern connecting possession belief and witchcraft beliefs is observed in both societies. However, the evidence of connection between these two is much weaker than is the evidence for the African background of possession trance. Thus, while history gives us information about how certain beliefs, rituals, and institutions developed over time and where some of them came from in a society made up, originally, of immigrants, it cannot give us a full explanation for the existence of these institutions. How then do society, and individuals, give rise to them, and how are they maintained? What do these institutions do for the society and for the individuals?

The Society

We must return then to our first question: Just how exceptional and unusual is Haitian possession-trance behavior? Admittedly, vodou, as it exists in Haiti, is a product and expression of that society, both of its past and its present. But what of the recurrence of possession trance—is it limited to African and Afro-American societies? What kind of information do we have

---

[1] A Cuban student at Ohio State University a few years ago proposed to write a paper on vodou (or a vodou type of) religion in Columbus. He could not believe that, with a sizable black population, such practices were, nonetheless, absent. Not content with his instructor's denial, he sought information from the surprised staff of the local newspaper, only to be disappointed, though not convinced. Even so, one may encounter what is called "voodoo" or "hoodoo" in the United States: practices of magic, curing, divination, the use of various potions and recipes. Many of these are indeed of African origin and have more recently been reinforced by Caribbean imports. And Haitian vodou centers do now exist in New York and Miami.

that could shed some light on such a question? In a recent study (Bourguignon, ed., 1973b), we found that both possession trance and possession
belief unrelated to trance are extraordinarily widespread throughout the world
among traditional and so-called "primitive" peoples. In our investigation of a
sample of 488 societies from all parts of the world we found some type of
possession belief in 360 societies (74%). Possession trance was found in 251
societies, or 52% of our sample. These percentages varied somewhat among
the various world regions: in sub-Saharan Africa, possession trance appeared
in 66% of our sample societies, and the lowest percentage (25%) having such
belief and behavior was found in aboriginal North American Indian societies.
This distribution certainly makes the Haitians seem considerably less special
and unusual, and a hypothesis of "racial psychosis" would surely appear less
than appropriate to explain their behavior. We must look elsewhere.

Two kinds of questions arise as we pursue this matter of an explanation: If
possession trance is practiced in 52% of our sample societies, how are these
societies different from those where it does not exist? And within these
societies that have possession trance, how are the individuals who practice
these behaviors different from those who do not? Let us take these questions
one at a time.

We may begin by taking a closer look at sub-Saharan Africa. Here,
working with a sample of 114 societies, Lenora Greenbaum (1973b) found
that possession trance there was significantly related, in a statistical sense, to
the presence (or recent presence) of slavery, and to the presence of a system
of stratification (two social classes or more) among freemen. She concluded
that there was apparently some relationship between fixed status distinctions
and social differentiation on the one hand, and possession trance on the other.
She proceeded, then, to inquire whether this relationship had something to do
with societal complexity in traditional societies or with societal rigidity of
some sort. She therefore pursued this matter in a further, descriptive analysis
(1973a).

Her argument here was that complex societies were likely to be more rigid
than simpler nonstratified ones, and that in a rigid social structure, where
individuals have little opportunity for achievement and little control over their
daily activities, possession trance is more likely to occur. The findings
appeared to support this hypothesis to the extent that simpler societies were
also more flexible and that rigid societies did in fact more frequently have
possession trance; yet more complex stratified societies are not necessarily
found to be rigid. The argument suggested here is this: Possession trance, by
offering a decision-making authority in the person of a medium, revealing the
presumed will of the spirits, allows persons oppressed by rigid societies some
degree of leeway and some elbow room. As such, possession trance may be
said to represent a safety valve, of sorts, for societies whose rigid social
structures cause certain stresses.

By Greenbaum's criteria, is Haiti now, and has it been since independence, a rigid, complex society? Certainly, it is a stratified society, a large-
scale state, more complex than any of the traditional African societies used in
the sample. In spite of periodic talk of democracy, the differentiation between
a small elite and the masses is deep-seated. Even though many of the mulatto
elite left the country during the Duvalier years, the gap between the small
French-speaking literate segment of the population and the vast illiterate
Creole-speaking mass still exists. Mobility is slight, even though Mintz
(1966) refers to the emergence of a small Creole-speaking literate, educated
class. For the great majority of the population, social position is ascribed.
The political system, in spite of its democratic constitutions, has generally
been autocratic, indeed since 1957 more nearly despotic. The political reality
is one of a hierarchically organized state. Thus with respect to social status
and political organization the system appears to come down rather heavily on
the rigid side. On the other hand, there is no fixed residence or membership in
a residential group, and many Haitians have moved from rural to urban
centers and from smaller towns to the capital. There are no restrictions on
travel; women traders, in particular, cover great distances every week as they
repeatedly attend centralized markets. With respect to religion, there is
officially freedom of worship, although at various periods vodou has been
excluded from this constitutional provision. Yet under Duvalier it practically
became the state religion; the dictator apparently used the existence of cult
centers as a basis for the development of a power network.[2]

The Individual

Within the vodou community, there is no centralized authority and each
houngan and each family appears to operate in terms of his, or its, own
tradition. Rites evolve over time, largely at the—supposed—will of the
spirits. As with migration and population movements, group membership is
not fixed, yet family and cult group exercise considerable influence over an
individual's life. Thus, with respect to this second group of criteria, Haiti
appears relatively less rigid than many African societies. Yet the oppressive
poverty, the domination of the masses by a small, centralized power group,
frequent hunger and illness, these are constant themes of a society organized
in strict hierarchical arrangements, from top to bottom. Here the leveling
effect of "institutionalized envy"[3] must be mentioned. Such envy is ac-
knowledged in the fear of being bewitched or of being accused of witchcraft.

---

[2]See Mintz (1966) mentioned above, as well as Courlander and R. Bastien (1966).

[3]E. R. Wolf (1955). A similar idea is expressed in G. Foster's concept of "the limited good"
(1967). Erasmus (1961) specifically refers to Haitian fears of bewitchment in speaking of what
he terms "insidious sanctions."

Thus, economic success and political success are objects of suspicion and good luck must be hidden or covered up. There is little trust among neighbors, and even some suspicion of relatives. A popular saying has it that one knows who people are in the daytime, but one cannot tell what they turn into at night. Illness and death of children are often blamed on werewolves (women who turn into a type of vampire). With respect to such dangers, the loa are important protectors. And in local thought the money one spends on rituals in their behalf is, therefore, good investment. Such expenditures also serve to reduce one's assets, acting as a leveling force, the while announcing one's formidable supernatural protection to any potential witch. Rituals also act to strengthen ties among members of cult groups or families, and between the faithful and their leaders.

In the political realm, Schaedel (1966:xii) speaks of the "feared Chef de section, the rural appointive representative who may hold sway over as many as 20,000 souls and occasionally emulates a rustic satrapy based upon a hierarchy of unsalaried aides and a dispersed harem."

As we have seen in the description of the Christmas rites, health, fertility, death, and magic are dominant themes in vodou ritual and they well express powerful anxieties. Fertility, it should be added, is important because of the high infant and maternal mortality. It is important also because having children gives a woman, particularly a common-law wife, some rights and some influence. Illness and death, particularly of children, are often blamed on witchcraft, believed to be motivated primarily by jealousy. On the other hand, we also find in these rituals expressions of power strivings, that is, of a search for compensation and self-respect among men humiliated in their daily lives. In possession trance there also appear to be opportunities for sexual expression and for the acting out of intimate interpersonal conflicts. Thus, while Greenbaum focuses on the importance of the decision-making functions of possession trance in rigid societies, functions that provide the individual with some alternative sources of authority, we can also see here the possibility of expressing and ventilating some unconscious stresses and conflicts and of deriving some satisfactions and compensations within the ritual framework. Also, we find that where persons are possessed spontaneously, in situations of stress, the spirits who possess them represent a defensive force whose help is depended on in moments of danger. The spirits, furthermore, may give orders and require activities which concern either others (as in Greenbaum's hypothesis) or the "horse," that is, the possessed person. Thus, in the role of the spirit, the individual may exercise some control over his own life or over those around him. This is true not only while the supernatural role is being played but also far beyond the moment of possession trance itself through commands and instructions and their consequences.

Admittedly, these supernatural interventions will not carry weight in one's relations with the police or the state, with an upper class employer, or with the tax collector. And here we have a significant difference between Haiti, where vodou is essentially a lower-class folk religion, and traditional African societies, such as for example that of the Fon of Dahomey, where the cults were indeed at the center of social and political power. Yet in spite of this limitation, within the peasant's world of other peasants, family members, cult-group members, neighbors, and peers these supernatural sanctions are still of considerable importance. In psychological terms, it may well be that we are here dealing with a type of behavior one might term "regression," but as I have suggested elsewhere (1965), to the extent that this regression permits the individual a wider field of action on his own behalf, we may more properly speak of "regression in the service of the self." Of course, this is not to say that we have here an explanation for all instances of Haitian spirit-possession trance. Yet at least some cases are accounted for in this manner. And the idea of a safety valve still remains valid here, for the society and for the individual as well.

Among various theories concerning possession trance which have been applied to Haiti is one by I. M. Lewis (1971), who considers vodou to be an "amoral peripheral spirit cult." Lewis, too, starts out from the reference point of African societies. In his ethnographic work among the Somali, he studied the existence of the *sar* cult. The Somali are a male-dominated patriarchal Islamic society of herders. Women are peripheral to all religious and political activities and powers. The *sar* is a type of spirit believed to possess women, causing illness. When such illness is diagnosed by a *sar* practitioner, the patient must have a ceremony performed for her, during which possession trance is induced. The troublesome spirit is questioned as to his identity and his wishes. These often center about ceremonies and initiation for the woman and gifts to the spirit, or his "horse." (The Somali, like the Haitians and many other people, consider the possessed person the mount of the spirit.) Lewis sees this type of possession cult as part of the "sex-war" between men and women. It is a way in which illness and therapy can be used to gain certain ends by the powerless and socially depressed, specifically by the women. Such spirit-caused illness may relieve a woman of some amounts of work or may cause her husband to spend on her money he might have invested in acquiring another wife. The spirits involved here are amoral, and peripheral to the dominant religious system of the society, namely Islam; the peripheral position of the spirits, says Lewis, reflects the peripheral position of the women in the society. He sees the peripheral cults as a form of "oblique aggressive strategy" by the powerless against the powerful. The reason, then, that women predominate in such cults (not only among the Somali, but in many other societies as well) is that they are the powerless in these societies. Where some types or categories of men are the powerless, they too will appear in peripheral possession cults, and they will be possessed by peripheral, amoral spirits. Lewis (1971:127) considers such religions to be "protest cults" and explains his view that

. . . possession is concerned essentially with the enhancement of status. The effect of possession by those spirits which we have classed as "peripheral" is indisputably to enable people who lack other means of protection and self-promotion to advance their interests and improve their lot by escaping, even if only temporarily, from the confining bonds of their allotted stations in society. Onerous duties and obligations are cast aside as those concerned seek refuge in clandestine cults which, since they are represented as cures, can be reluctantly tolerated by the established authorities.

Following this line of reasoning, Lewis suggests that Haitian vodou for the most part fits this category of cults, for he sees it as a religion of the subjugated and dominated. It is undoubtedly true that "status enhancement," in a number of senses of the words, is, as we have seen, relevant to an understanding of vodou. The political and economic handicaps of the Haitian peasantry also cannot be disputed. Yet to me it seems rather incorrect to place vodou in Lewis's category of "amoral peripheral possession" cults. Nor is vodou now a protest religion, even if it may have had that role at one time in Haitian history. Vodou, incorporating as it does many elements of Catholicism and of an ancestor cult, seems rather to be a "central morality" religion in Lewis's terms. Only some of the spirits may be considered "amoral" or "peripheral"; on the contrary, the major spirits are indeed upholders of morality. Furthermore, in vodou possession illness is not a prelude to cult membership. The illnesses the spirits cause, if any, are *sent* by them, not produced by possession. Here it is noteworthy that Lewis does not point to what seems to me to be a most notable aspect of the East African cults: the transformation of the spirits in their relation to their human hosts as a result of initiation into the cult. The initial possessions are considered illnesses, involuntary, fearful. They may involve an involuntary first possession trance. Ritual initiation leads not only to controlled, voluntary possession trance and the cure of the illness. It also transforms a harmful dangerous spirit into a helpful one, an ally. Where involuntary, illness-causing possession in Europe and in India leads to exorcism, in these East African cults it leads to an accommodation with the possessing spirit. In Haiti, quite in contrast, although some harmful spirits may be banned, the majority of the loa are acquired by the individual through family ties or cult group. There is no transformation of the spirit from a harmful to a helpful agent. The spirits generally are seen as protectors, as long as their rules are obeyed, rules that involve moral as well as ritual prescriptions.

Lewis is interested in two aspects of what he terms "amoral peripheral" possession cults, and he appears to group both of these under the heading of "status enhancement." The distinction, which seems of some importance, is not made explicitly by him. One aspect refers to the status-enhancement satisfactions derived by the individual in possession trance. One satisfaction is in the acting out of the fantasy of superior, powerful roles; another is in the ability through this acting-out to compel the attention and the efforts of other individuals perhaps more powerful than the self, who must carry out the wishes of the spirits in order to make possible the patient's cure. Here we are no longer dealing with fantasy, but with real effects on the individual patient and on her male relatives as well. In contrast to this aspect of possession trance is the effect of the cult structure, indeed of the very existence of the cults themselves. The cults offer to certain individuals within them positions of relative power and authority, an alternative ladder of achievement, even access to wealth. To some extent, these positions then become relevant to the total power structure of the society.

In spite of important differences from the Somali *sar* cult, these considerations apply to Haiti to some extent. The possession trancer in Haiti is not a patient in the sense that an illness is believed to be caused by possession or even that initiation is generally preceded by illness. There is no good evidence that initiation is paid for by worried relatives, on whom pressure is brought to bear. However, it is true that, on the one hand, some expressive satisfaction is gained from fantasied temporary "status enhancement"—as well as from other expressions of emotions and needs. Also, the individual, as already noted, may be in a position to affect the behavior of others over a longer term, as well as to affect her own situation vis-à-vis others. On the other hand, there is the cult structure itself, which offers avenues to wealth and power to the able, of influence over others, even of some political influence. To many men who are not themselves houngans, it offers positions within the cult hierarchy, whether or not they ever experience possession trance.

In a society where money is scarce and mobility limited, these cults are important avenues to relative power, money, and prestige. It must be remembered that Haiti has been for all its history a society that is basically divided into two parts: a small upper class of essentially Western and specifically French cultural orientation, and a large mass of the people steeped in a traditional world view and way of life to which African traditions have contributed heavily. The official political structure is imposed on the people and, in many respects, is remote. It offers few services, if any, to the masses. The peasants' social behavior is sanctioned by others of their own class and within this class, the vodou priests and priestesses and their cult societies play a prime role. They oppose evil and offer protection against it and they impose obedience; through magic, they offer manipulation of the system. Within the universe in which the cult groups operate, the manifestation of the spirits through possession trance is of key importance. Yet the quasi-political role of the priests must be distinguished from the personal functions that possession trance has for the individual.

So far, we have seen that, according to Greenbaum's two statistical and descriptive studies (1973), we may expect, at least with reference to Africa, to find possession trance institutionalized in societies with fixed status distinctions. This expectation fits the Haitian picture. Furthermore, we may expect possession trance to serve as a decision-making alternative in rigid societies, giving individuals options not otherwise open to them, because mediums act as the mouthpieces of the gods and speak with the authority of the gods. This expectation too makes sense in the Haitian setting. I would add, however, that it is not only the medium who can make decisions for a client; the possession trancers can affect their own lives as well as those of others. Lewis (1971), as we have seen, perceives possession trance primarily as a vehicle of status enhancement—either because the cults offer positions of relative power or influence or because the individual can be another, more powerful self during the possession trance. He perceives in particular those cults which he terms "peripheral amoral" possession cults as offering both satisfactions to the oppressed and means of attack in a battle between unequal forces. In Haiti, however, the possession cult offers power within the oppressed class but only to a very limited extent in the total social structure. Also, as was noted, while the vodou cult may offer "status enhancement" this appears not to be the whole story, for needs other than prestige strivings are expressed and satisfied.

The fact, however, that the cults fulfill both a social function as well as an individual one does not show us how individuals do in fact enter the appropriate states. How does the fact that possession trance plays an important role—in the operation of the society and of the cult groups, and in the lives of the individual actors themselves—relate to the individual's experience of possession trance, to his (or more often to her) appropriate behavior in the right time and place?

The Experience

We have already noted that Dorsainvil (1931) saw such behavior as pathological. Even if so, this behavior is related, as we have seen, to certain factors of social structure; this is clear from our statistical findings. Herskovits (1937b), in contrast to Dorsainvil, argued to the contrary, that possession-trance behavior was culturally approved and rewarded, culturally learned, and consequently normal; only by non-Haitian standards could it be considered pathological. More recently, Nelida Agosto Muñoz (1972) has spoken, with respect to vodou, of the "social control of the unconscious." To her, possession trance is to be understood as involving the psychological mechanism of dissociation. However, the personality that appears in a state of dissociation is one that results from learning during the process of initiation. Thus, where Dorsainvil saw only the idiosyncratic in possession trance, Agosto goes a step further than Herskovits. In fact, she seems to argue that there is no personal element involved here. According to her, the individual's secondary personality which asserts itself in dissociation in response to certain cues is a socially imposed personality. Several points are involved here: (1) cultural learning— this is clearly evident in the high degree of shared patterning visible in possession trance; (2) the concept of dissociation, and indeed regression in psychological terms, which offers an understanding of how such alterations in personality are possible; (3) the notion that this behavior is not the result of individual pathology in spite of its similarity to the multiple-personality syndrome sometimes seen in patients in Western society.

Multiple personalities represent a dramatic psychological phenomenon, which has great popular appeal, if one is to judge by the success of the book and film *The Three Faces of Eve* (Thigpen and Cleckley, 1957) and, more recently, by the best-seller *Sybil* (Schreiber, 1973). In this report of an authentic case, we discover a woman with no less than 16 personalities, including two that are male! Each of these has a name and a variety of distinguishing personality characteristics. Sybil is amnesic for these others although they are aware of her and to some extent of each other. The great difference between such a patient and the characteristic Haitian cult initiate (or for that matter, a possession trancer in any of our 251 sample societies and many others as well) is that these dissociations are purely idiosyncratic; the behavior is not learned by following a cultural model. No one has attempted to teach dissociation to Sybil; to her associates it can only seem weird and bizarre and not the ordinary behavior of familiar and recognizable spirit entities. In Haiti, dissociation into diverse (spirit) personalities fits in with the understanding people have of the universe, of gods, and of human nature. In the United States, it does not. Here we expect a person to be "himself," to be predictable and consistent, and we are alarmed when behavior does not fit expectations.

The case of Sybil and of other multiple personalities shows that the potential for dissociation is present in many individuals and in many societies —not only in societies where this capacity, or potential, is culturally utilized and institutionalized, encouraged, and rewarded, or institutionalized and penalized (as in societies where demonic possession trance is feared and abhorred), but also in societies that seem to ignore the possibility of such "splits" in personality altogether.

When we compare the situation of the victim of the multiple-personality syndrome in Western society and the Haitian possession trancer, the differences are striking. Cultural learning is of primary importance here, as is the induction of the behavior by specific cues (drum rhythms, songs, dancing, ritual setting) on appropriate ritual occasions. However, if we reconsider the description of the Christmas ritual presented earlier, it is clear that Agosto (1972) overstates the case: we have noted personal as well as cultural factors in the symbolism of the possession-trance behavior. Also, over time a single person may act out a series of spirit personalities whose characters have different meanings for her, or him. And most importantly, the individual is initiated only for a single one of these entities. Thus, the learning that takes place in the initiation process does not account for all the initiate's possession-trance performances. Furthermore, although there is similarity in the perceived personalities of a given spirit from individual to individual, and in the same "horse" from occasion to occasion, there is also variability and individuation. In other words, the behavior is not highly stereotyped.

In contrast to Haiti, the Dahomean and Yoruba cults, as well as the orthodox Afro-Brazilian cults of Bahia,[4] present a greater degree of stereotypy; an individual is possessed only by a single spirit, and initiation may last as long as a full year. In Haiti, by contrast, it may last from three to seven days.

And the very fact that an individual's first possession trance is usually spontaneous and involuntary suggests the personal psychological roots of this behavior. This point has been stressed by Ravenscroft (1962), who noted that first possession trances generally occur at adolescence, suggesting a crisis of individual development. He relates this to some observations about Haitian peasant child training—that infants are indulged but that children are treated quite harshly, with disobedience punished by beatings. When the child grows up and attempts to assert himself as an adult, he experiences unconscious conflict over this behavior, for which he had been previously punished. This conflict is expressed in a first possession trance; this in turn results in a reorganization of the personality, helping the individual in his acceptance of appropriate adult behavior. It is indeed striking that children are hardly ever seen to experience possession trance and that the phenomenon is relatively rare in older people. To the extent that it occurs in young people, it is part of learning the appropriate cult-related roles and part of learning adult secular roles as well.

Since a discontinuity between childhood behavior and adult behavior is to some extent universal, to make a definitive test of this hypothesis would require a statistical study of the relationship between possession trance and the Haitian type of child-rearing patterns. Yet it seems to me that the discontinuity that Ravenscroft notes is less striking than another aspect of Haitian life—its essentially hierarchical organization. In the hierarchy small children must obey those older than themselves, but they must assume responsibility for even younger children, whom they may beat as their elders

---

[4]For a striking photographic essay, showing the continuity between Brazil and West Africa, see P. Verger (1954). See also M. J. Herskovits (1966).

beat them. Similarly, adults are expected to be obedient to those either senior or superior to them. There is no time when the individual is fully submissive and dependent and no time when he or she is fully dominant and independent. This pattern is acted out in the person's relations to the spirits as well as to human authorities. In this respect it is not surprising that people may address male spirits as "papa" and that spirits may address women as "my wife."

However, one aspect of submission-dominance seems of importance in relation to possession trance: the person, as we have seen, is said to be "mounted" by the spirit, to be his "horse." The personality of the individual, one of his souls called "gros bon ange," is displaced and the body is taken over by the spirit. In other words, there is total subjection to the spirit and total submission to him (or her). The spirit, as a powerful superhuman entity, can do as he pleases, both with the horse he has mounted and with other human beings present. We thus have an expression of extreme passivity in this interpretation of possession trance. Yet, if we as objective observers consider the behavior of the spirit to be in fact the behavior of the individual himself, acting out, unconsciously, the role of a spirit, we see great expressions of aggression, mastery, self assertion, authority, and the likes. Women assume the roles of males and men those of females. Thus, we might translate this observation as follows: Possession trance offers alternative roles, which satisfy certain individual needs, and it does so by providing the alibi that the behavior is that of spirits and not of the human beings themselves. And furthermore, in order for human beings to play such assertive roles, they must be totally passive, giving over their bodies to what are ego-alien forces. In a hierarchical society, demanding submission to those in authority, one acquires authority by identification with symbols of powers, identification which goes as far as the total assumption of the other's identity, total loss of one's own. In this authoritarian society, it is possible to act out dominance fantasies by pretending, to self as well as others, total passivity and subjection.

Another aspect of the possession-trance phenomenon in Haitian vodou must, however, not be lost sight of, namely its theatrical element. As Métraux (1959) has stressed for Haiti, and M. Leiris (1958) for the zar cult of Ethiopia, there is a great deal of play acting in the dramatic structure of possession-trance ritual. The interactions among spirits may amount to impromptu playlets. Skilled actors can portray a variety of personalities and the depth of trance is not readily testable. It would seem, from observation, that there is great variation in depth of dissociation in a single individual over an extended period of time, in one individual from occasion to occasion, and among individuals. The subject who experiences possession trance with more frequency comes to experience it with greater ease, with less disturbance, and with more control over the process. Also, the more knowledge of the experience is acquired, the greater the control. The Haitians recognize these facts when they say that the greater esoteric knowledge a person acquires the more rarely will he be possessed. Yet, although the line between theatrical acting and dissociated acting out is at times a thin one, an observer should not expect to find widespread simulation. For the mass of the faithful, simulating would seem a dangerous thing to do, a behavior which the gods might avenge. Furthermore, even when dissociation is genuine and of considerable depth, the individual must remain in contact with his environment and sensitive to a variety of cues. Possession trance, it must be remembered, is a public manifestation; it occurs among observers and it requires an audience. This audience offers the spirit role of the actor a variety of stimuli to which he must respond: greetings, food and drink and tobacco, music, questions to be resolved, and more. All of these require attention, if only selective attention. The phenomenon is in great contrast to the hallucinations of a drug-induced type of trance, where the primary events are intrapersonal private experiences, not interpersonal public transactions. It should be stressed, therefore, that possession trance is not induced through drugs, alcohol, or other biological or biochemical factors. In fact, when F. Huxley (1966) experimented by giving an experienced mambo a dose of LSD, she did not go into possession trance but hallucinated a conversation with one of her loa.

Summary

To conclude our discussion of Haitian vodou, then, we may say that we have here an institution whose roots go back into the African past of the people. It has survived, because it has adaptive value for the people and for the society. The people find it possible to play the requisite roles and to have the appropriate experiences, however, not only because cultural learning of this behavior is available but also because they have the personality structures, resulting from their particular upbringing and life experiences, that make them apt to engage in such behavior and to find it personally as well as socially rewarding.

4

POSSESSION BELIEF AND POSSESSION TRANCE: SOME CONTRASTS

We began by contrasting possession trance with the type of possession belief that is not expressed in an altered state of consciousness. We noted that most human societies have some type of belief in spirit possession and that in just over half the societies in our sample this belief finds its expression in possession trance. In many societies, too, two or more forms of possession belief exist, at least one of which is expressed in possession trance and one not so expressed. We have found an example of the coexistence of these two basic types in the Haitian vodou tradition. We earlier compared societies having possession trance with those that lack it, and have found, at least with respect to Africa, that they tend to be fairly complex societies, likely to have slavery and a class system. We may now compare societies that have possession trance with societies having a different type of possession belief.

Types of Societies

As was mentioned earlier (see page 31 above), we carried out an extensive comparative study on hundreds of societies. Specifically, we analyzed and tabulated information on 488 societies, in all parts of the world, for which information on a variety of aspects of social life was available to permit us to carry out statistical comparisons. For the purpose of these comparisons, societies having both possession trance and a form of nontrance possession belief are grouped together with those having only possession trance, and contrasted with those having possession belief of a nontrance type only. Societies having no belief in possession—as far as we could tell from published reports—are excluded from this analysis. The results of this comparison are rather intriguing, and we shall attempt to account for them presently.

42

The characteristics with reference to which we carried out our comparisons are the following: (1) A society's degree of dependence on a particular type of subsistence economy (hunting, gathering, fishing, agriculture, animal husbandry); no industrial societies are included in our sample. (2) A society's typical settlement pattern (that is, nomadic, seminomadic or sedentary). (3) The size of the society's population, that is, both the size of the local group and of the larger unit to which it belongs (tribe, ethnic group, or other). (4) A society's political complexity as expressed in its jurisdictional hierarchy. (5) And finally, a society's social stratification in the form of a division into classes or the presence (or recent presence) of some form of slavery. The information required for this analysis was taken, in somewhat modified form, from Murdock's *Ethnographic Atlas*.[1] As a result of our tests, we find that, in statistical terms, these two groups of societies are significantly different—that is, the difference is not due to chance—on at least six major interrelated points.[2] (For the sake of simplicity, in the following discussion we shall call the possession-belief-only societies P, and the possession-trance societies PT.)

1. P societies depend on a combination of hunting, gathering, and fishing for 46% or more of their livelihood. PT societies are more heavily dependent on agriculture and/or animal husbandry for their subsistence.
2. As might be expected of people whose livelihood is based on hunting, gathering, and fishing, P societies are more likely to be nomadic or seminomadic, while PT societies tend to be sedentary.
3. These P societies are relatively small; local groups have a mean size of less than 1,000. Local groups in PT societies tend to be larger.
4. The same scale relationship holds for the overall size of the societies (tribes, ethnic groups, and the like): the P societies are likely to have an estimated overall population of less than 100,000 and the PT societies again tend to be larger.
5. These small-scale P societies are not likely to have a jurisdictional hierarchy above the local level; that is, decision making and leadership reside in the band or community, not in a tribe or state. For the PT societies, larger in numbers, sedentary in settlement pattern, the opposite is true. They are more likely to have a jurisdictional hierarchy extending beyond the local level.

---

[1]The *Ethnographic Atlas* (Pittsburgh University Press, 1967) contains, in coded form, a great quantity of information on 863 societies in all parts of the world. Our sample was drawn from this larger total. To make the comparisons reported here we simplified and reorganized the codes of the *Atlas* somewhat. For a detailed review of the *Atlas* as well as for an explanation of our codes, see Bourguignon and Greenbaum (1973).

[2]As measured by chi-square, which is significant below the .001 level.

6. Our small-scale P societies are unlikely to have a class structure or slavery; the PT societies, as we have already been led to expect by Greenbaum's African study, are more likely to have both.

In brief, we see that in economy, in settlement pattern, in population size, and in political and social organization, P societies are on the whole less complex than PT societies. We must say "on the whole" and "are likely to be" because we do not have a one-to-one association here between these various factors. Migrations and historical connections tend to upset the tidy pattern of interrelationship one might expect. Moreover, we find some exceptions to show that such terms as, for instance, "hunting, gathering, and fishing" may conjure up somewhat unrealistic pictures. An example may be helpful here.

On the Northwest Coast of North America, in British Columbia, we find a group of American Indian tribes who are widely known for their spectacular art, particularly their totem poles. These people, including the Kwakiutl, the Haida, the Tlingit, and a number of others, lived primarily by fishing. Their fishing was of a somewhat special sort: they controlled the headwaters of the salmon rivers, so that they had a large assured annual catch, and they developed techniques for preserving fish and oil. They were wealthy, had slavery and class stratification, and lived in compact towns. The glory of their families was expressed in their crests, the famous totem poles. They had secret societies, and possession trance of a dramatic sort was practiced among them. Clearly, this is not the kind of hunting, gathering, and fishing society that comes to mind when the words are mentioned: people whose fishing is seasonal, for example, such as the Indians of the Eastern Woodlands of the United States and Canada, and who for most of the year depend on hunting and gathering. Under certain special circumstances, fishing can give a substantial economic base for the development of more complex societies, with enough to spare to support a nobility, accumulations of wealth, and political hierarchies.

In view of these considerations, then, it must be remembered that we are speaking in terms of probabilities only and not describing each and every PT society when we speak of complexities, or each and every P society when we speak of relative simplicity. Yet an approach of a statistical sort is in some respects preferable to one which deals only with a handful of societies, for the accidents of selection then can lead us into the making of generalizations based on what may be, for the most part, special and exceptional cases.

If we take another look at our statistics, it seems clearly to make sense that what are basically hand-to-mouth economies—requiring movement over sizable territories to provide enough food—can support only relatively small populations. It seems in turn that these small societies do not need the kind of social and political organizations—and could not afford them—that wealthier and larger societies have and need. Nor is there in such simple societies enough wealth to allow for the types of status differentiation involved in slavery and class differences. Yet, even though we may see the interconnection of these factors, we still do not have a clue as to why one of these types of societies, the more complex one, is more likely to have possession trance while the other, the simpler one, is more likely to have a possession belief not expressed in trance. We need to consider this matter more closely to see whether differences between P and PT give us some hints as to why this difference should exist.

Nontrance Possession

We have earlier considered some examples of possession belief not linked to possession trance. These referred to illness, or deformity of several types, whether among the Haitians or among the cases cited in the New Testament. However, such belief may also be connected to at least two other categories of phenomena: power and witchcraft. The power belief is particularly characteristic of the aboriginal peoples of the Americas, the witchcraft belief of various parts of Africa. Let us cite some examples: According to Colson (1953), among the Makah Indians of the Northwest Coast of North America, who seem not to have had a possession-trance complex, power entered into a person, giving him the ability to cure. According to Opler (1940:65-143), among the Southern Ute Indians, shamans are said to have "inside themselves . . . a tiny 'being' which directs the use of the power and [it] is the one that swallows the sickness" which the shaman draws out of his patient. For the Teton, Dorsey (1889-90:495) tells us that they believed a shaman had a "mysterious being dwelling within himself" which enabled him "to practice medicine." Many other North American examples could be cited. In South America, too, we find over and over again that the ability of the shaman to cure derives from the presence inside of him of a power or spirit.

We noted earlier that a belief in spirit possession, often spoken of as "spirit intrusion," is widespread as accounting for various types of illness. Sometimes this spirit is thought to assume the form of an animal. The belief in a more or less personified power residing in the shaman, which enables him to cure, is then, in some sense, the reciprocal of that idea. The shaman uses his power for socially desirable ends (although he may also cause harm). The converse of his curing power is found in the idea that witches, too, have a "being" inside of them, which causes them to do harm. This notion is widespread in Africa. Witches, in this view, are persons who, sometimes unbeknownst to themselves, harbor such a witchcraft spirit or being. This being is activated by jealousy and causes harm. The human host of this being may not be aware of harboring it, he may not intend harm, he performs no actions or manipulations, uses no "black art." He does have conscious, or perhaps even unconscious, bad thoughts. The witchcraft being inside of him does the rest. One example among many others of this type of belief is found among the Fang of West Central Africa (Fernandez, 1961). The presence or existence of the witchcraft is tested for in an autopsy, when a witch or suspected witch dies.

All these possession phenomena are quite different from possession trance, as we have already seen. For one thing, while there is, by definition, an altered state of consciousness in the case of possession trance, such a state does not exist in the other types of possession. Possession trance is a state of relatively brief duration, from a few minutes to a few days at the most. Possession, whether illness, power, or witchcraft, may in contrast last for a lifetime or most of it. In possession trance, during the altered state, the individual loses his or her identity for the duration, an identity which is replaced by that of one or several other personalities, wills, or spiritual entities. This alteration is not the case for the other types of possession: the self, the personality, the identity are unchanged. Whereas some aspects of the self are replaced or displaced by possession trance, in nontrance possession something seems to be added to or modified in the self or person of the individual: he experiences illness, which constitutes a diminution of his powers in some sense, or he experiences an increase in his powers, either for good, as in shamanism, or for evil, as in witchcraft. He does not lose his self to have it replaced by that of another; rather, the qualities or capacities of the other modify the self.

Furthermore, possession trance and nontrance possession belief vary with respect to other dimensions as well. Possession trance is behavior, culturally patterned, occurring within acceptable cultural limits, yet it is expressive to a greater or lesser degree of various drives, strivings, needs, emotions, and the like. Unconscious as well as conscious aspects of the personality are drawn into this essentially public behavior, with an alibi that the behavior is that of the possessing spirit. Nontrance possession, however, refers to a belief concerning capacities or states of the individual, a belief often held primarily not by the individual but by others concerning him, as a diagnosis or as public opinion. In respect to shamanistic power it may be a claim or assertion made by the individual concerning his skills, his qualifications to practice medicine.

The Concept of Self

These differences apply not only to the social function of the beliefs and behaviors, but also to the concept of self that people hold: the manner in which the self may be modified, its consistency through time, its relations with beings and forces outside the human realm. Now, conceptions of the self are cultural products, as are other beliefs, and these may be expected to make sense in terms of the total way of life of a people. Ideas about one's own self are acquired by the individual in the process of growing up in a particular society. Among the aspects of this development of the self are ideas and evaluations concerning self-reliance, independence, achievement, or, on the other hand, the acceptance of responsibility, obedience, and concern with others. What then do we know about the child-training patterns of the societies which concern us?

Barry, Child, and Bacon (1967) raised the question of whether there is a relationship between methods and goals of child training and the characteristic subsistence economy of a society. They reasoned that child training prepares for adult roles and, specifically, for adult economic roles. Here, they felt, there must be differences among societies on the basis of "the extent to which food is accumulated and must be cared for." Among people who live by herding as well as those who live by agriculture, routines and rules of economic behavior are part of the tradition of the society, part of its accumulated knowledge. Because of the great risk to food supply, then, independence, experimentation, and innovation will be discouraged. Adults must be reliable individuals, taught to accept responsibility and the care or nurturance of animals or plants; they must be obedient to their seniors and to social rules. Children may be expected to have these virtues inculcated in them from an early age, by punishment as well as encouragement. On the other hand, the situation of hunters or fishermen, with little provision for storing their catch, is entirely different. These people live in terms of short-range risks and immediate successes. They may often be on their own as individuals and must have appropriate self-reliance, independence, initiative, and achievement motivation. Child training, particularly for boys, will prepare them for such adult roles.

To test their hypotheses, the authors of this important study selected a sample of 104 traditional, nonindustrial societies around the world and, on the basis of published reports, studied their subsistence economy and their child-training methods with respect to the variables of responsibility, obedience, and nurturance, which together are termed "compliance," and the variables of achievement, self-reliance, and independence, which together are termed "assertion." They found their hypothesis strongly confirmed, so strongly indeed that they conclude (p. 254): "a knowledge of the economy alone would enable one to predict with considerable accuracy whether a society's socialization pressures were primarily toward compliance or assertion." Yet there are also differences among the sexes, with the pressures toward compliance generally greater for girls than for boys, regardless of the type of economy (Barry, Bacon, and Child, 1957).

Now the types of societies which exert strong pressures for compliance are also those where we expect to find possession trance. The types of societies which exert strong pressure toward assertion are those for which we expect to find nontrance possession beliefs. The personalities and value systems developed in a society may be expected to be consistent with the conditions of livelihood and social organization which people face. And these in turn are reflected in their ideas concerning spirits and powers which constitute their religious beliefs. In societies in which one succeeds by being obedient, responsible, and nurturant, in short by being compliant, we may expect that such behavior appropriate toward elders and those in power will also be appropriate toward powerful spirit beings. The individual enhances his power and his status by total abdication and self-effacement before the spirits. He abandons his body to them as their mount; his spirit vacates its place before them. He can achieve dominance and assertion only indirectly, through the unconscious pretense of obedience and submission. On the other hand, the shaman who acquires power, and the witch as well, do not impersonate spirits, do not abdicate their own identity; even the patient who is diminished in some sense by spirit-intrusion illness remains himself. Those who through some form of possession acquire powers for good or for evil have these powers supplement their own; their selves are strengthened rather than displaced. A shaman's chances for achievement are enhanced by the acquisition of spirit power. His relation with the spirit is not dependent on the group; rather, he has most likely obtained it on his own, in his own dealings with the spirit. Nontrance possession represents an alteration of the individual's capacities, not an alteration of his consciousness. In societies which socialize for assertion, such an alteration of capacities results from the interaction of independent, self-reliant human beings with spirits or powers of limited capacities.

A cautionary note should be introduced here: although most human societies do have some form of possession belief, 26% of our worldwide sample do not; among North American Indian societies, those without any form of possession belief amount to a full 48%. Possession belief is a human invention and in some societies this invention was either not made or not adopted. Yet there are other ways of communicating with spirits in ritual contexts: among the Indian societies without possession belief, all but one had a pattern of ritual trance, mostly of a hallucinatory or visionary type, in which communication with spirits could be established. And this type of communication, in contrast to possession trance, also correlates with hunting and fishing economies and a pattern of socialization for assertion rather than compliance.[3]

Summary

It is suggested here, then, that there is a relationship between the complex of economy, social organization, and child-training practices and the complex of religious beliefs and practices, specifically beliefs concerning possession of human beings by spirits and the ways in which this possession is manifested. These beliefs and behaviors reflect the patterns of social interaction in

---

[3]For a more detailed discussion of this point, see my essay *Culture and Varieties of Consciousness* (1973a).

the society, the values prized and taught to children, and the personalities that individuals develop in the process of growing up in particular kinds of societies. Possession beliefs and rituals then reflect and express both social structures and the personalities of the participants. They are not simply matters of historical inheritance. When such inheritance loses its social significance and profound personal psychological meaning, the beliefs will disappear and possession-trance rituals will become theatrical performances.

5

POSSESSION BELIEF AND POSSESSION TRANCE IN WESTERN HISTORY, THEN AND NOW

Some Examples from History

We saw in our introduction that the subject of possession is a popular theme in contemporary entertainment. Yet it also has some profound meanings to many people in our society. Possession belief, manifested in a variety of ways, appears both in the Hebrew and Greek roots of Western society; and these early sources of our traditions had their own connections with the traditions of other peoples and other parts of the world. This point is of some importance, for there is an easy temptation to see Western traditions as somehow radically different from—and superior to—those of so-called "primitive" peoples. Yet the roots of both traditions and the basic psychological needs in both are surely the same. An example of such a connection can be found in the fact—as E. R. Dodds (1957), the famous classical scholar, points out—that the Delphic oracle of Apollo, with its oracle priestess the Pythia in possession trance, has ties to the ancient traditions of shamanism of Northern Eurasia. This oracle is an interesting case to consider in the light of the views of I. M. Lewis (1971), who sees women's cults as reflecting their marginal position and who expects to find men in possession trance in those official state religions that he calls "central morality cults." In the Greek instance, we have a clear case of official religion, yet a woman is the oracle. However, in support of Lewis, it must be noted that the apparently somewhat incoherent ramblings of the Pythia were interpreted by male priests, probably to conform to some policy lines.

The case of the Dionysian cults was different. Here, if we are to believe

Euripides, we have a cult of women who are temporarily "driven mad" by Dionysus. How frequent or widespread these phenomena were—and some have considered them inventions of the poet—we do not know. But it is interesting that Dodds finds it useful to study the inferences provided by the dramatist in the light of cross-cultural information on primitive and traditional societies. Similarly, the French classicist Jeanmaire (1951) found it useful for his analysis of the Greek cults to draw specifically on the *zar* cult of Ethiopia for a comparison. The information available to us about the Greek cults is tantalizingly slight; comparison suggests what some of the allusions may refer to—for example, how frenzied dancing to the sound of drums might be related to healing in a cult of women. The suggestion made here is that the Greek cults, like the *zar* cult, were curative and that the cure involved the induction of possession trance. Perhaps, then, in the Greek cults also some accommodation with the possessing spirits was worked out. Such ideas were in great contrast to the idea of possession by evil spirits that we find in the New Testament, where the treatment for the disorder is the exorcism of the spirits believed to cause it.

The Jews of the time of Jesus apparently had acquired much of their belief in great numbers of demons from the Parsees; at least at the level of orthodox rabbinical interpretation, they did not think of the possessing demons as entirely evil but rather as subject to God, even as his agents of punishment. This view explains in part the ready acceptance of the idea that Jesus, and other exorcists of the times, could drive demons out in the name of God. (That the cures performed by Jesus were not considered as unique and totally surprising is illustrated by the criticism leveled against him that he had broken the Sabbath by performing cures, thus implying that his healing was work, like other kinds of work.) The demons of the Jews were usually demons of something specific—of an unclean place, of death, of corpses, of cemeteries, of ruins, of the desert, of a specific symptom of illness, the demon of asthma for example. This fear of uncleanliness, here concretized in the fear of demons, is expressed in the Old Testament prohibition against a priest's defilement by death, a prohibition that forms part of the background of the Parable of the Good Samaritan. The deserted unclean places, even latrines, are still places of danger in the Arab world, where jinns and afrit dwell, who may seize and possess a person, causing illness or madness.

But to return to the Jews and the period of Jesus: While the New Testament holds that evil spirits caused harm through possession, the sophisticated view of the day, expressed by such writers as Flavius Josephus and Philo Judaeus, was that possessing spirits were really souls of wicked dead men, and Josephus spoke of a special root which can be used to expel them (1960:V, 6; 260-261). Guignebert (1959:103) suggests that "there were probably manuals for the would-be exorcist, in fact a whole mass of literature" in existence at the time.

These traditions of cure of various types of illness continued through antiquity and the Middle Ages. They were codified in the various Christian churches, in Judaism, and in Islam, and their remnants are still very much with us. Jews developed belief in a type of possessing spirit, called dybbuk, who was the soul of a dead person, usually a sinner. To cure the victim, the dybbuk had to be exorcised in a dramatic ritual.[1] In the Christian tradition, in time, these beliefs and practices became tied to some aspects of witchcraft beliefs, as in the example of the contemporary Alsatian case (Israel and North, 1961), cited above.

Witches, themselves, unlike the African ones we mentioned earlier, were generally not thought to be possessed. Rather, it was believed that they had made a pact with the devil and had thus acquired power to harm others; they might, for one thing, cause individuals to be possessed. Interestingly enough, as in the African case, envy was often thought to be the primary motivation of witchcraft (and of witchcraft accusations as well).

The principal sign of possession rarely was illness; more often it was blaspheming and obscenities spoken through the mouth of the possessed person by the possessing spirits. The possession constituted an alteration of the consciousness and will of the victim; in our terminology this is a type of possession trance. The spirits had to be exorcised. The best-known examples of this type of behavior come to us from France; the most famous is the case of Jeanne des Anges and her nuns at the convent of Loudun, a case which has been published in detail and analyzed and studied over and over again.[2] Here first the prioress and later a number of other nuns believed themselves to be possessed by demons sent by a witch, Father Urbain Grandier, who was executed for his supposed crime. Even the exorcist, Father D. D. Surin, appears to have fallen victim to the hysterical contagion. The most famous case in America is undoubtedly that of the witches of Salem (Hansen, 1969). Here, too, there was a connection between supposed witchcraft activities and possession, although the victims were not possessed by demons but by the spirit of the witch herself. There was no need to search for a suspect here; the victims knew by whom they were possessed.

With respect to Salem, it is interesting that there existed a link with another cultural tradition, the African one, in the person of a black West Indian slave woman.

Possession was only one aspect of the historical phenomenon of witch-craft, with its persecutions, tortures, confessions, trials, and executions. In fact, at some times and in some places possession was probably a minor

---

[1]See the impressive first-hand description by Frommer (1812) of an eighteenth-century case as cited by Oesterreich.

[2]The most famous of these studies is undoubtedly Aldous Huxley's (1952). A more recent one is a study by Michel de Certeau (1970).

aspect, if it was present at all. Alan Macfarlane (1970), for example, finds only a few references to possession caused by witches in the records of a 120-year period of English history between 1560 and 1680. Strikingly, when a band of exorcists appears on the scene, he finds that then there is reference to possession. It is as if the exorcists had raised this issue in the minds of the people, and had thereby stimulated the development of the evil they were out to fight. Suggestion is ever powerful in the development of such states!

However, even though possession beliefs and accusations may have been at times only minor features of the witch fears and persecutions, from the point of view of our discussion the connection is of importance. It is reminiscent of the case of the Zulu, among whom also some types of possession illness are thought to be due to spirits sent by witches.

We may now compare the principal features of European and American types of demonic possession with what we have seen in other societies. The periods of witch persecutions to which they correspond on the whole are indeed periods of social stress and conflict. Societies were undoubtedly rigid, with little individual freedom. Yet contrary to the Greenbaum hypothesis based on African studies and discussed earlier, possession trance, as we have described it for Europe, does not provide for the individual a spirit medium as a decision-making authority. The African and Afro-American patterns of possession trance are of a totally different sort compared to the one seen here. Nor is it clear how this demonic type of possession trance allows for status enhancement, as Lewis would have it. It does allow the victim to attract attention and enables him or her to cause harm—directly in the American case, indirectly more generally in the European case—to the person who is suspected and accused of having caused the bewitchment.

Personal and Cultural Elements

Most sources that attempt to deal with the demonic-possession phenomenon in explanatory terms focus on the personal aspect, the pathology of the victim, the essentially hysterical character of the attack. If we assume that spirits or devils are not actually active in the case, the source of the obscenities and blasphemies that are uttered must be a dissociated or split off part of the person himself, or herself, a part that the conscious personality represses and disowns, and is indeed horrified at. This reasoning fits in with the picture of the possession trancer that we have arrived at earlier: a person who is seen by others, and who sees himself, as the passive victim or vehicle of aggressive spirits. In these hysterical attacks the materials that are expressed are ascribed to the possessing spirits. They may involve hostility against religion, commonly blasphemy; hostility against others, as in witchcraft accusations; or such other tabooed and repressed materials as sexual fantasies. In a sense, these attacks, manifested by one who knows consciously that they will be followed by exorcism, simultaneously demonstrate a breakthrough of the repressed feelings and constitute an appeal for the help of the community or its authorities in dealing with the overwhelming force of the individual's own contradictions and the anxieties which they produce. These unconscious conflicts constitute a hysterical illness, for which the exorcistic rituals provide a culturally sanctioned type of therapy. They may, however, also constitute suggestions for the development of the illness along characteristic lines.

Yet, without denying the obviously psychopathological aspects of the cases that can be studied, the anthropologist must be impressed by the importance of cultural elements in this syndrome. For example, as we have already mentioned, in Protestant New England, the witch's spirit possesses the victims—not devils, as in Catholic France. And in the Jewish cases of possession, the dybbuk is the spirit of a dead person. Furthermore, in the Christian cases the possessed are the innocent victims of a mean witch. In the Jewish possessions no witch is involved; the dybbuk acts on his own. But, in the interesting case cited by Oesterreich and mentioned earlier (Frommer, 1812, in Oesterreich, 1966), and this is an important point, the dybbuk announces, through the mouth of his victim in the course of the exorcistic proceedings, that he was able to enter into her because she had illicit sexual relations. Thus, the exorcism includes a public announcement of guilt and the possession may well be interpreted as a punishment for this guilt.

Wallace (1966:143-144) speaks of possession as "socially sanctioned alteration of identities" and sums up his discussion by saying: "Salvation by possession, then, involves the *acceptance* of two (or even more) mutually contradictory identities, each being permitted, or even encouraged, to take exclusive control of the body at certain times, with more or less mutual ignorance or indifference."

Possession beliefs, as we have seen, existed (as in the time of Jesus) prior to and independently of the witchcraft persecutions and panics. Among Jews, witch belief was not connected with the possession concept. With witchcraft as a major concern essentially out of the way since the eighteenth century, possession belief has yet survived. Those who claim to be witches or Satanists nowadays do not appear to provoke demonic possession hysterias. In the contemporary beliefs, again, it is the evil spirit who chooses his victims, not a witch who selects them. Nowadays, possession belief still appears in a number of contexts, quite aside from the frequent use of the theme of demonic possession in fiction. Rituals of exorcism of various churches still exist. Blatty, for example, has claimed that his novel *The Exorcist* (1971) is based on an authentic case of Catholic exorcism in Washington, D.C. The spiritual healing of many of the Pentecostal and Holiness churches, and others, in this country is based on the idea that illness is of the devil and that driving out the devil is healing the patient. In the matter of speaking in tongues (or *glossolalia*), of which more in a moment, one hears comments by preachers that if the tongues come at inappropriate moments, as for example during the sermon, there is some question as to the sources of the phenomenon, that it may not be of the Holy Ghost but may instead be of the devil who wishes to disrupt the service.

In quite a different context, the subject of possession also comes up, namely the missionary context, when Christians come into contact with people who have a religious tradition of possession trance. In Haiti, for example, missionaries of various persuasions have attempted to teach that the spirits which possess human beings in vodou ritual are devils or demons. Some use strong persuasion to drive out these spirits, and their methods of powerful suggestion are, often enough, effective. I recall hearing of a Pentecostal preacher who hit people on the head with the Bible. The head being the seat of the loa, they were driven out, he said, by this book with powerful words in it. In this kind of interpretation of traditional religions, non-Christian people are turned into devil worshipers! (Although the Haitian vodouists consider themselves Catholics, and vodou impossible without Catholicism.) As to the success of some of these missionary pressures, D. H. Salman (1968:184) has pointed out, "A white man's belief in the Devil simply reinforces and confirms the native's trust in his own spirits and deities."

Pentecostalism and Glossolalia

There is also a positive side of possession belief in Christianity, namely the idea of being "filled" with the Holy Spirit. It is based, in particular, on the account of the Pentecost (Acts 2), when according to the text the Holy Ghost descended on the apostles and bestowed on them the gift of tongues. That is, they preached to a multitude in languages they themselves did not know. This tradition, together with other "manifestations of the spirit," has been of importance in various strains of Christianity from time to time, bursting forth in periods of religious revival.

In the history of the United States at various critical junctures possession trances have appeared in the Christian churches, for example in the Great Awakening and the Kentucky Revival (see M'Nemar, 1846), in the development of Negro churches, in the growth of Protestant Pentecostalism toward the end of the nineteenth century, and currently in the neo-Pentecostal or Charismatic movement. We may take a brief look at these last two. Little is in effect known about the specific origins of Protestant Pentecostalism. It is a characteristically American phenomenon; it developed among both black[3] and white poor, in relatively isolated rural areas. Some would argue that the specific ecstatic behavior represents an influence of transformed African traditions among whites. Pentecostal cults are religions of salvation, with

---

[3]See the classic study by Arthur Huff Fauset (1971).

dramatic conversions, spiritual healing, group participation in ritual, singing and music, sometimes dancing, but generally a broad range of motor behavior. Some even handle snakes and others drink strychnine in proving their true faith.[4]

In the late 1950's speaking in tongues spread to some of the established Protestant denominations first, later to some Catholic university students. In the major denominations this dramatic behavior was seen among many with alarm. As Virginia Hine (1969:224) has put it:

In a society where the public display of emotion is reserved for spectator sports, and where the appropriate background for spontaneous and uninhibited self expression is the cocktail party, the abandonment of one's self to a joyous flow of unintelligible vocalization and possibly some non-consciously controlled physical behavior is considered indecent if not insane.

Such behavior appears to be learned[5] and, in Hine's view, constitutes a sign of commitment to a converted life. The late James Pike, as Bishop of the Episcopal diocese of California, appointed a Study Commission on Glossolalia, whose 1963 *Report* dealt with the theological and psychological issues of this new development. It is clear here that this behavior, in the context of the present study, can be called "possession trance" only if the participants consider themselves to be "possessed," not if some other explanation is offered for the behavior. As the authors of the *Report* state on the basis of interviews with glossolalists (Diocese . . . Report, 1963):

All agree . . . that a measure of control is given up [to the Holy Spirit] for what is said is not pre-determinable by the individual nor is he able to duplicate what he has said once he has finished.

Neo-Pentecostalism is basically a middle-class movement. Its members are derived from the established churches and do not have a familiarity with the Pentecostal behavior in their background. They include a broad range of Protestants and, more recently, a significant number of Catholics as well. Their first experience with speaking in tongues is a dramatic event for them and formalizes their conversion and commitment. But as Pentecostalism spread from the uneducated poor into the middle class, a number of changes and transformations occurred.

In contrast to the lower-class traditional Protestant Pentecostalists, the

---

[4]See, for example, Weston La Barre (1962). Also, see the excellent documentary film: *Holy Ghost People*, filmed in Appalachia in 1966-1967 by Peter Adair.

[5]For a detailed discussion of glossolalia, its linguistic features, the learning of the behavior, its cross-linguistic consistency, development over time, etc., see Goodman (1972).

Charismatics' behavior is subdued and restrained. There is no dancing, no dramatic motor behavior such as jumping or rolling about on the ground, no extravagant behavior such as snake handling or strychnine drinking. In spite of their great commitment, the class differences between the groups are clearly evident. At first, the so-called Jesus Movement attracted attention on the nation's campuses in particular. For at least some of these young people, enthusiastic Christianity, like some of the Eastern religions, appears to have constituted a halfway house from the drug culture. At this point, it is not possible to understand this turning of middle-class youth to ecstatic religion apart from the general broader picture of the contemporary youth culture and youth crisis. It is interesting to observe that there is such a crisis among adults as well and that to some extent the charismatic movement appears to be filling a void. It is certainly too early to foresee whether it will have a lasting effect on American religion and what that effect may be.

It may be of interest to stop for a moment to compare these enthusiastic Christian religions, and their concept of possession by the Holy Spirit expressed in more or less profound and elaborate states of possession trance, with the demonic possessions discussed earlier. The demoniacs appear to have been individuals suffering from culturally stereotyped states of hysterical illness. They were able to act out some parts of their repressed and dissociated emotions and anxieties, although it appears they could not act out more fully developed alternate personalities in the manner of the possessed in Haitian vodou. The case of the Pentecostalists is still different. Here, in terms of the prevailing beliefs, all glossolalists or all those actively involved in some form of altered state of consciousness are believed to be possessed by or filled with the Holy Spirit, not by individual differentiated personalities. They may develop more or less individuated patterns of glossolalia and more or less individuated motor patterns, but little else to mark off their own uniqueness. They are likely to act in concert, glossolalia or dancing being appropriate for all so inclined at some particular time during religious services. The activity is collective, but the experience is private. Relatively little communication with their fellows is involved, although where ecstatic prophecy is practiced or where glossolalia is conceived of as containing a message to be translated, attention by the group to the message is forthcoming. The primary recipient of collective attention is the group leader, who may also help in the induction of the ecstatic behavior of others, preach, perform healing activities, or lead prayers. Among traditional Pentecostalists, where individuals grow up in an environment that encourages the appropriate beliefs and behaviors, there is, it would appear, no reason to expect to find gross pathology, of the kind involved in demonic possession. Boisen (1939) and Wood (1965) among others have provided evidence to show on the one hand the difference between Pentecostalists and psychiatric patients, and on the other the "normalcy" of such enthusiastic Christians as indicated by their responses to a personality test.[6]

In the case of the middle-class Pentecostalists, there appears to be even less opportunity to act out individuality of patterning. The behavior is generally subdued and the ecstatic, uncontrolled expression of emotion is apparently somewhat de-emphasized. Yet these people, unlike the Appalachians, are deviants from the norms of their peer groups, a fact which they express by becoming members of the Charismatic movement; this affiliation tends to express their dissatisfactions with the patterns of life and religion to which they are accustomed. As a result of their middle-class background, however, they practice their Pentecostalism in a relatively subdued manner, more generally in conformity with their general lifestyle.

It should be kept in mind, however, that this middle-class development in the United States is only one example of the expansion of Pentecostalism. Indeed Pentecostalism appears in the 1970's to be one of the two most rapidly spreading religious movements throughout the world. The second of these movements is spiritualism (or spiritism). And both of these movements involve some form of possession trance.

Some Other Contemporary Possession Religions

Pentecostalism is spreading rapidly in Latin America,[7] where it is spawning a series of local developments and variations. F. D. Goodman (1973) has reported on the fascinating case of one such local development. Among the converts of a small Yucatec village, religious enthusiasm grew over a period of several months with the great conviction of the imminent end of the world. There was much ecstatic behavior, beginning with the spread of glossolalia and active motor behavior in possession trance; there were prophecies and eventually visions, including visions of the devil, hysterical outbursts and accusations by teenage girls, a general high pitch of excitement. Eventually, after mass baptism and fighting with visions of Satan, the excitement subsided. Church authorities outside the village were consulted and some order was reestablished. The excitement was said to have come not from the Holy Ghost but from the devil who acquired a new reality for the group.

There is some similarity between such groups and movements and the many separatist churches that have grown up throughout Africa. Some of the elements of the traditional possession-trance cults are integrated into these Afro-Christian churches. For example, among the Zulu (Sundkler, 1961), possession trance is believed to come from the Holy Ghost, but curing is

---

[6]Note, however, that La Barre in his study (1962) of snake-handling cultists sets forth considerable evidence of the psychological peculiarities of some of the cult leaders.

[7]See, for example, C. Lalive d'Epinay (1968).

carried on by the diviners as it was of old. Such syncretic religions, combining elements of Christianity with traditional native beliefs, are widespread, and, indeed, we have a fully developed example of syncretic religion in Haitian vodou. They are one way in which peoples throughout the world attempt to come to terms with westernization and the problems it creates for them.

Another type of spreading possession religion is spiritism, or spiritualism. The key element of this belief system consists in the claim that the disincarnate spirits of the dead may communicate with the living through human mediums, persons with particular gifts for such contacts. This movement is usually claimed to have begun in the United States in the middle of the nineteenth century, whence it spread to the British Isles and to the European continent. In a formal sense, there exists a religion of Christian Spiritualists who founded the Greater World Christian Spiritualist League in 1920. However, there are many independent spiritualist "churches" in most American cities. In addition, the Frenchman L. H. D. Rivail (1804-1869), writing under the pseudonym Allan Kardec (1878), developed a syncretic system combining elements of spiritism, of Hinduism (especially the concepts of reincarnation and karma), of Catholicism, and some ideas of his own. It is this branch of spiritism which is currently spreading throughout Latin America. In Brazil, it has contributed heavily to the development of Umbanda, a modern religion which combines African, Catholic, Indian, and spiritist elements (Pressel, 1973). It has a substantial following, particularly among the educated.

Pedro McGregor, a Brazilian journalist and himself the founder of the Temple of Universal Religion, has described these varieties of Brazilian religion, including a chapter on the much publicized case of spirit medium José Arigo, who is reported to operate successfully with a kitchen knife when possessed by a spirit of a dead German physician by the name of Fritz (McGregor, 1967).

Kardecism has also formed an element in the development of the modern Vietnamese religion, Caodaism. It was founded in Saigon in 1926 by Ngô Van Chiên, combining elements of Catholicism, Buddhism, and Kardecism in the attempt to develop a universal religion. It borrowed some of its organizational structure from Catholicism, with the establishment of its own pope and with the recognition of saints, among whom are included such notable modern figures as Victor Hugo.

Needs and Satisfactions

These modern syncretic religions appear to address themselves to a variety of needs. Among these is a need to integrate the great mass of beliefs and the claims of the many religions which people in contact situations encounter. The type of intellectual integration, of course, varies with the amount of information available and the educational level of the participants. Other types of needs as expressed by both spiritualism and Pentecostal religions have to do with the healing of physical illness in societies where medical care is inadequate and where the stresses of life lead to a variety of psychosomatic disorders. Furthermore, in spiritist religions, as is seen in the examples of Brazilian Kardecism and Umbanda in particular, mediums—or their spirits— provide explanations and advice for a large number of personal problems, as Pressel has documented in detail. Thus, the hypothesis Greenbaum had developed for African societies is generally supported by the information on these religions. The problems, here, however, appear to arise not primarily or exclusively from the rigidities of the complex Brazilian society but by the rapid changes and dislocations which people experience. In such situations of disorientation, the mediums provide a source of guidance and, importantly, an authority on which one may rely. Also, there is evidence in support of Lewis's hypothesis of the importance of the enhancement of the individual's status as a medium in spiritism and as a preacher and leader in the Pentecostal churches. In fact, there appears to be plenty of opportunity for abuse in such positions of power and influence, as indicated, for example, by Marjoe Gortner in his filmed revelations concerning his life as a child evangelist. An interesting review is presented by La Barre (1970) in his chapter on "The False Messiahs," which shows both the secular rewards and the psychic rewards of these would-be leaders.

It is true that for the followers the satisfactions differ somewhat from those available to the leaders. It is important to note that where people are able to act out a range of personalities and roles, as in spiritism, what we have said for the varieties of dissociated tendencies in the individual in the case of possession trance still holds. However, in Pentecostalism, the situation appears to be somewhat different. There, for the followers primarily, the personal satisfaction of assurance of salvation and the cathartic aspects of the experience are of importance; there is also, for some, the knowledge that others are aware of their conversion and of their new selves. On the other hand, particularly among middle-class neo-Pentecostals in the United States, there is little individuation of behavior in possession trance and indeed the existence of an altered state of consciousness is de-emphasized. In a society where conformity is at a premium, it may well be that the new group the individual joins in his search for salvation provides him with new rules of conformity, after he has broken, to some extent, with some of the rules of his former peers.

The British psychiatrist Sargant has drawn an analogy between ecstatic religious conversions and political conversions described as "brainwashing" (1957). He explains both of these phenomena in terms of Pavlovian psychology as due to a forgetting of previous learning as a result of a high pitch of excitation and a new learning in the resultant state of high suggestibility.

Although this is a striking explanation for single conversion experiences, it does not account for people who engage in possession trance over and over again, whether in vodou, in spiritism, in Pentecostalism, or in the many other types of possession-trance religions that exist.

It may be, as the sociologists Glock and Stark (1965) have argued, that particular kinds of "deprivation" encourage the development of religious movements. They phrase their terms very broadly, suggesting that deprivation consists of "any and all of the ways that an individual or group may feel disadvantaged in comparison either to other individuals or groups or to an internalized set of values" (p. 246). Just what kinds of deprivations are involved in particular cases is not always clear. They are likely to differ from society to society and among different social groups and classes within the same society. Max Weber (1963) has argued that such religious exaltation is characteristic of the first formative stages of religion, and that later, routinization of behavior and ritual set in. Furthermore, during these formative periods there is a greater equality of the sexes and ecstatic religious expression is open to women as well as to men. Religions of this revival type appear in times of social stress and as society becomes structured, formal organization takes over. Presumably, and Lewis follows Weber here, the inspirational type of religion could present a source of instability to a stable society and an organized religion. From the point of view of the present discussion, we may note that such inspirational religions may involve the concept of possession trance, or in quite a different way, the inspirational source of the religious message may come in the form of a prophet's vision. In fact, it appears from a review of what La Barre (1971) has termed "crisis cults" that most of these reactions to the trauma of social disruption involve some type of claim to supernatural inspiration. Yet the majority appear to involve not possession trance but altered states of a different, visionary type. When mass possessions appear, as in the Yucatec example described by Goodman, in the Kentucky Revival on the American frontier, or in the Vailala Madness of Papua (Williams, 1923) these are relatively short-lived phenomena that appear to burn themselves out fairly rapidly. When possession trance is, however, fully institutionalized, as in Haiti, in the Umbanda cult of Brazil, or in the many other cases that we have mentioned, the situation is quite different. Here, through the function of the medium, the door is left open for innovations of a relatively controlled sort. Where the behavior of the medium is fully stereotyped, on the other hand, no innovation is to be expected and possession trance operates in highly formal purely ritualistic terms only. A good example is seen in the case of the West African Kalabari as described by Horton (1969). Here a man annually plays the possession-trance role of one of the founding ancestors in a highly stereotyped manner. The man is forced to accept this rather difficult assignment. On the other hand, there is a type of spontaneous possession trance among women, whose behavior is much less stereotyped, whose spirits make various kinds of prophetic statements, and through whom innovations may come into the society.

On the whole then, possession-trance cults as they exist in our own society, in the form of neo-Pentecostalism and to some extent spiritualism, are signs of crisis, expressions of needs. They do not appear to be solutions to the problems of society. They are expressions of anxiety, together with many of the other signs that abound. The interesting aspect of all of this is primarily the observation that under certain types of stress many individuals will not only turn to religion for help, but specifically to types of religious forms that appear to provide profound emotional catharsis and the kind of conversion experience and commitment that reach deep into the person's unconscious. The individual abandons his conscious control over his self temporarily in psychologically regressive behavior to allow what he believes to be a more powerful force to take over his body and his tongue and to act through him. It is characteristic that possession-trance groups of the traditional Pentecostal types have strong leaders, to whom the followers are attached by complex feelings of gratitude and obedience. It will, therefore, be interesting to see what kind of leadership the neo-Pentecostals develop.

Weston La Barre (1970) has suggested that societies develop religions in response to the unmet needs of their people. It is characteristic that in contemporary America, neo-Pentecostalism has developed at the same time as other forms of ecstatic religion and other types of abdication of rational control, among them drug cults and various forms of Eastern mysticism. To understand the religious developments, then, we must look at the total society and at its points of stress. It is clear that technology and rationality have not delivered on their promise. A retreat from reason and a retreat from accepting responsibility for one's own life decisions are evident in the growing number of groups that claim authority over individuals on the grounds of religious revelations and convictions. It will be interesting to see whether these old ideas in new dress represent a temporary fad or indicate a major redirection of American culture as is claimed by some of their advocates.

6

A BIBLIOGRAPHIC NOTE

As we have seen, beliefs in possession are very widespread indeed. As a result, the literature on this subject is vast; a very large number of anthropological reports on individual societies contain at least some reference to this subject. Studies that deal specifically with religious beliefs, rituals, traditional medicine, and a variety of other subjects are likely to go into the matter in some detail. In spite of all of these specific studies, there are relatively few general works dealing with the broader perspective, and providing the reader with a theoretical framework to put some order into the myriad of specific details and observations.

The classic work on the subject is still T. K. Oesterreich's book. Its full title is: *Possession, Demoniacal and Other, among Primitive Races, in Antiquity, the Middle Ages, and Modern Times*. It was first published in Germany in 1921, and it was translated into English by D. Ibberson. The first English-language edition was published in 1930. In 1966 it was reissued in America by University Books, Inc. Oesterreich was a philosopher and psychologist, who, at the time of the publication of his monumental work, was head of the Department of Philosophy at the University of Tübingen. The book covers an enormous literature, a good deal taken from the work of missionaries and explorers, psychiatrists, and historians as well as from original historical documents. The work of early anthropologists he cites is either no longer available or no longer read. Much of it comes from sources generally unfamiliar and inaccessible to the American reader. The author was interested in psychic (parapsychological) and psychological phenomena, but this interest in no way biased his treatment of sources. His ordering devices are a distinction into voluntary and spontaneous possession, a grouping of his cases by time periods, and a distinction between so-called "primitives" and "higher civilizations."

The book is invaluable for its collection of data. However, more than fifty years have passed since its publication and much additional information has been collected. Furthermore, from the point of view of the anthropologist, the broad cultural context is generally lacking not only in Oesterreich's compilation, but often enough also in his sources.

No one has again attempted such a broad collection of materials. However, a number of synthesizing and more highly analytic studies have been published, which may be of interest to the general reader as well as to the specialist. In particular we shall pay attention here to publications in English. It is important to distinguish, as we have done in the text, between (1) possession beliefs, including those which account for possession trance, and (2) various types of altered states of consciousness. Altered states which are accounted for by other types of explanations will not concern us here, although some of the studies to be cited do not make this distinction. I. M. Lewis, *Ecstatic Religion: An Anthropological Study of Spirit Possession and Shamanism*, published by Pelican Books in 1971, is a broad introduction to the general field, and although I do not find myself in full agreement with Professor Lewis, as the reader of this book will have discovered, this is an interesting volume, well worth investigating.

Africa, as we have seen, is undoubtedly one of the prime centers of possession-trance cults. John Beattie and John Middleton bring together a series of excellent descriptive studies in their edited volume entitled *Spirit Mediumship and Society in Africa* (New York: Africana Publishing Corporation, 1969). Most of their chapters provide specific cultural settings for the observations of possession-trance behavior. I. I. Zaretsky has put together a fine research tool in his *Bibliography on Spirit Possession and Spirit Mediumship* (Evanston: Northwestern University Press, 1967). This, too, deals almost exclusively with African materials, although some Afro-American references are included.

My own edited collection, *Religion, Altered States of Consciousness and Social Change* (Columbus: Ohio State University Press, 1973), attempts to sketch a broader canvas, including both statistical and original field studies in several world areas, and seeks to develop a framework for the analysis of altered states of consciousness in general. The descriptive material, however, focuses on possession trance in varying cultural settings. Another collective volume, tied together somewhat more loosely and treating other varieties of altered states as well, is *Trance and Possession States*, edited by Raymond Prince (Montreal: R. M. Bucke Memorial Society, 1968).

Some of the most extensive descriptive material outside of Africa concerns Haitian vodou. Here we must refer to the pioneer work of M. J. Herskovits: *Life in a Haitian Valley*, published originally by Knopf (1937) but reprinted by Anchor Books. This study treats the subject of vodou in dispassionate anthropological and historical terms, setting it properly in its cultural context.

This is in great contrast to the great volume of sensationalist writings which have both preceded and followed it. More recent and more detailed studies are to be found in A. Métraux, *Voodoo in Haiti* (New York: Oxford University Press, 1959). This too is now available in a paperback edition (New York: Schocken Books). This book, first published in French, unfortunately suffers from some lapses in the translation. H. Courlander's *The Drum and the Hoe* (Berkeley and Los Angeles: University of California Press, 1960) is an outstanding study by a close student of Haiti, and contains great wealth of information and excellent detailed observations.

The general Afro-American field is splendidly covered by R. Bastide in his *African Civilizations in the New World* (New York: Harper Torchbooks, 1971). Bastide is also the author of a number of very detailed studies, specifically on Brazilian cults.

A broad range of information on possession trance is available with reference to Asia, primarily in two regions, Southeast Asia and Indonesia, and to Northern Eurasian shamanism. Two of the most important works for the former region with respect to the materials covered here are Jane Belo's *Trance in Bali* (New York: Columbia University Press, 1960) and M. E. Spiro's *Burmese Supernaturalism* (Englewood Cliffs, N.J.: Prentice-Hall, 1967). Mircea Eliade's *Shamanism: Archaic Techniques of Ecstasy* (New York: Pantheon Books, 1964), although approached with some reservations by anthropologists, does for Northern Eurasia what Oesterreich does for the field as a whole.

Each of the works cited above includes voluminous references and extensive leads for further reading and study. Many aspects of the current American scene are covered in a volume edited by I. I. Zaretsky and M. Leone: *Religious Movements in Contemporary America* (Princeton University Press, 1975).

A word should be added here on the literary and fictional use of possession-trance materials. Its extent is truly striking and the interest which it appears to stimulate is astonishing. For example, Marion Starkey, who published an excellent historical study of the Salem witch trials in her book *The Devil in Massachusetts* (New York: Knopf, 1949), has recently published an account of the same subject for children 12 and up, entitled *The Visionary Girls* (Boston: Little, Brown, 1973). Arthur Miller's play *The Crucible* is also based on the Salem witch trials. Aldous Huxley's nonfictional *The Devils of Loudun* (New York: Harper, 1952) was referred to above. It has been turned into a play by John Whiting, an opera by Krzysztof Panderecki, and a highly controversial film by Ken Russell. One of the most famous fictional literary treatments of the subject of demonic possession is S. Ansky's Yiddish play, *The Dybbuk*. The English version was first published in 1921, and was reissued in paperback (New York: Liveright, 1971). It attained world-wide fame in the stage and film version by Israel's Habimah theater. In 1974 a ballet by Jerome Robbins and Leonard Bernstein was based on it. Paddy Chayefsky's play *The Tenth Man* was originally titled *The Dybbuk in Woodhaven*. A recent advertisement in the *New Yorker* tells us that, "The author of *The Possession of Joel Delaney* has written a new novel of possession, terror, and exorcism . . . *The Apparition* by Ramona Stewart." In the present mood of readers it appears that the subject of possession combines terror, suspense, violence, and the uncanny in just the right proportions.

REFERENCES

Agosto Muñoz, Nelida 1972. "Haitian Voodoo: Social Control of the Unconscious," *Caribbean Review* 4:6-10.

Ansky, S. (Solomon Rappoport) 1921. *The Dybbuk.* Later printings: New York: Boni & Liveright, 1926. New York: Liveright: 1971.

Balicki, A. 1970. *The Netsilik Eskimos.* Garden City, N.Y.: Doubleday/Natural History Press.

Barry, H., III, M. K. Bacon, and I. L. Child 1957. "A Cross-cultural Study of Some Sex Differences in Socialization," *Journal of Abnormal and Social Psychology* 55:327-332.

Barry, H., III, I. L. Child, and M. K. Bacon 1967. "Relations of Child Training to Subsistence Economy," in C. S. Ford, ed., *Cross-Cultural Approaches: Readings in Comparative Research.* New Haven: HRAF Press. Originally published in *American Anthropologist* 61:51-63 (1959).

Bastide, R. 1971. *African Civilizations in the New World.* New York, Harper Torchbooks.

Beattie, John, and John Middleton, eds. 1969. *Spirit Mediumship and Society in Africa.* New York: Africana Publishing Corporation.

Beckman, D. M. 1974. "Trance: From Africa to Pentecostalism," *Concordia Theological Monthly* 45:11-26.

Belo, Jane 1960. *Trance in Bali.* New York: Columbia University Press.

Blatty, W. P. 1971. *The Exorcist.* New York: Harper.

Boisen, A. 1939. "Economic Distress and Religious Experience," *Psychiatry* 2:185-194.

Bourguignon, E. 1965. "The Self, the Behavioral Environment and the Theory of Spirit Possession," in Spiro, ed., 1965.

Bourguignon, E. 1967. "Religious Syncretism among New World Negroes," printed in major part in Whitten and Szwed, eds., 1970, pp. 36-38.

Bourguignon, E. 1973a. *Culture and Varieties of Consciousness.* Reading, Mass.: Addison-Wesley Module in Anthropology No. 47.

Bourguignon, E., ed. 1973b. *Religion, Altered States of Consciousness, and Social Change*. Columbus: Ohio State University Press.

Bourguignon, E., and L. S. Greenbaum 1973. *Diversity and Homogeneity in World Societies*. New Haven: HRAF Press.

Certeau, Michel de 1970. *La Possession de Loudun*. Paris: Julliard.

Chayefsky, Paddy 1960. *The Tenth Man* (Original title *The Dybbuk in Woodhaven*). New York: Random House.

Colson, E. 1953. *The Makah Indians*. Minneapolis: University of Minnesota Press.

Courlander, H. 1960. *The Drum and the Hoe: Life and Lore of the Haitian People*. Berkeley and Los Angeles: University of California Press.

Courlander, H., and R. Bastien 1966. *Religion and Politics in Haiti*. Washington, D.C.: Institute for Cross-Cultural Research.

Deren, Maya 1953. *Divine Horsemen: The Living Gods of Haiti*. London and New York: Thames and Hudson.

Diocese of California, Episcopal Church, Division of Pastoral Services, Study Commission of Glossolalia 1963. *Preliminary Report*.

Dodds, E. R. 1957. *The Greeks and the Irrational*. Boston: Beacon Press. Original publication Berkeley: University of California Press, 1951.

Dorsainvil, J. C. 1931. *Vodou et Névrose*. Port au Prince.

Dorsey, J. O. 1889-90. *A Study of Siouan Cults*. Bureau of American Ethnology, *Annual Reports* 11:351-553.

Eliade, Mircea 1964. *Shamanism: Archaic Techniques of Ecstasy*. New York: Pantheon.

Erasmus, Charles J. 1961. *Man Takes Control*. Indianapolis: Bobbs-Merrill.

Fauset, Arthur Huff 1971. *Black Gods of the Metropolis: Negro Religious Cults in the Urban North*. Philadelphia: University of Pennsylvania Press. Original publication, 1944.

Fernandez, J. W. 1961. "Christian Acculturation and Fang Witchcraft," *Cahiers d'Etudes Africaines* 2:244-270.

Foster, G. 1967. *Tzintzuntzan*. Boston: Little, Brown.

Freud, Sigmund 1923. "A Neurosis of Demoniacal Possession in the Seventeenth Century," in *Collected Papers of Sigmund Freud*, vol. 4. London, Hogarth Press, 1953.

Frommer, Jacob 1812. *Ghetto-Dämmerung, Eine Lebensgeschichte*. Leipzig: 3d ed. Cited in Oesterreich (1966).

Glock, C. Y., and R. Stark 1965. *Religion and Society in Tension*. Chicago: Rand McNally.

Goodman, F. D. 1972. *Speaking in Tongues: A Cross-Cultural Study of Glossolalia*. Chicago: University of Chicago Press.

Goodman, F. D. 1973. "Apostolics of Yucatan: A Case Study of a Religious Movement," in Bourguignon, ed., 1973b.

Greenbaum, Lenora 1973a. "Possession Trance in Sub-Saharan Africa: A Descriptive Analysis of Fourteen Societies," in Bourguignon, ed., 1973b.

Greenbaum, Lenora 1973b. "Societal Correlates of Possession Trance in Sub-Saharan Africa," in Bourguignon, ed. 1973b.

Guignebert, Charles 1959. *The Jewish World in the Time of Jesus*. New Hyde Park, N.Y.: University Books. Earlier publication New York: Dutton, 1939.

Guthrie, George M. 1973. *Culture and Mental Disorder*. Reading, Mass.: Addison-Wesley Module in Anthropology No. 39.

Hansen, Charles 1969. *Witchcraft in Salem*. London: Hutchinson.

Hastings, James, ed. 1963. *Dictionary of the Bible*, revised edition ed. Frederick C. Grant and H. H. Rowley. New York: Scribner's. Original publication 1898-1902.

Herskovits, M. J. 1937. "African Gods and Catholic Saints in New World Negro Belief," *American Anthropologist* 39:635-643.

Herskovits, M. J. 1937b. *Life in a Haitian Valley*. New York: Knopf. Paperback reprint, Doubleday Anchor Books.

Herskovits, M. J. 1941. *The Myth of the Negro Past*. Boston: Beacon Press, 1958 reprint.

Herskovits, M. J. 1966. *The New World Negro: Selected Papers in Afroamerican Studies*, ed. Frances S. Herskovits. Bloomington: University of Indiana Press, 1971.

Hine, Virginia 1969. "Pentecostal Glossolalia: Toward a Functional Interpretation," *Journal for the Scientific Study of Religion* 8:211-226.

Horton, Robert 1969. "Types of Spirit Possession in Kalabari Religion," in John Beattie and John Middleton, eds., *Spirit Mediumship and Society in Africa*. New York: Africana Publishing Corporation.

Huxley, Aldous 1952. *The Devils of Loudun*. New York: Harper.

Huxley, Francis 1966. *The Invisibles: Voodoo Gods in Haiti*. New York: McGraw-Hill.

Israel, L., and E. North 1961. "Incidence médico-légale d'un délire de sorcellerie: exorcisme ayant entrainé la mort d'un enfant." *Cahiers de Psychiatrie 1961*. Summarized in *Transcultural Psychiatric Review* 15:64-67 (1963).

Janet, Pierre 1898. *Les Névroses et les Idées Fixes*. Paris: Alcan.

Jeanmaire, H. 1951. *Dionysos: Histoire du Culte de Bacchus*. Paris: Payot.

Josephus, Flavius 1960. *The Great Roman-Jewish War (De Bello Judaico)*. New York: Harper Torchbooks.

Kardec, Allan (L. H. D. Rivail) 1878. *Heaven and Hell*. London: Trubner & Co.

La Barre, Weston 1962. *They Shall Take Up Serpents*. Minneapolis: University of Minnesota Press. Also New York: Schocken, 1969.

La Barre, Weston 1970. *The Ghost Dance: The Origins of Religion*. Garden City, N.Y.: Doubleday.

LaBarre, Weston 1971. "Materials for a History of Studies of Crisis Cults: A Bibliographic Essay." *Current Anthropology* 12:3-44.

Laguerre, M., S.J. 1970. "Brassages ethniques et émergences de la culture häitienne." *Revue de l'Université Laurentienne / Laurentian University Review* 3:48-65.

Lantis, M. 1950. "The Religion of the Eskimo," in Vergilus Ferm, ed., *Forgotten Religions*. New York: Philosophical Library.

Lalive d'Epinay, C. 1968. *El Refugio de las Masas*. Santiago, Chile: Editorial del Pacifico.

Leiris, M. 1958. *La Possession et ses Aspects Théâtraux chez les Ethiopiens de Gondar*. Paris: Plon.

Lessa, W. A., and E. Z. Vogt, ed. 1958. *Reader in Comparative Religion*. Evanston: Row, Peterson.

70   REFERENCES

Lewis, I. M. 1971. *Ecstatic Religion: An Anthropological Study of Spirit Possession and Shamanism*. Baltimore: Pelican Books.

Leyburn, J. G. 1966. *The Haitian People*. New Haven and London: Yale University Press.

Macfarlane, Alan 1970. *Witchcraft in Tudor and Stuart England: A Regional and Comparative Study*. London: Routledge & Kegan Paul. New York: Harper.

McGregor, Pedro 1967. *Jesus of the Spirits*. New York: Stein and Day.

M'Nemar, R. 1846. *The Kentucky Revival*. New York: Jenkins Publications. (Originally 1807.)

Métraux, Alfred 1959. *Voodoo in Haiti*. New York: Oxford University Press. Paperback reprint, Schocken Books.

Michael-Dede, Maria 1973. "The Anastenari: From the Psychological and Sociological Viewpoint," *Thrakika* 46:153-180.

Miller, Arthur 1953. *The Crucible*. New York: Viking.

Miner, Horace 1960. "Culture Change under Pressure: A Hausa Case." *Human Organization* 19:164-167.

Mintz, S. 1966. "Introduction," in Leyburn 1966.

Oesterreich, T. K. 1966. *Possession, Demoniacal and Other, among Primitive Races, in Antiquity, the Middle Ages, and Modern Times*. D. Ibberson, tr. New Hyde Park, N.Y.: University Books. First English-language edition, 1930: original German publication, 1921.

Opler, M. K. 1940. "The Southern Ute of Colorado," in R. Linton, ed., *Acculturation in Seven Indian Tribes*. New York: Appleton-Century.

Opler, Morris E. 1958. "Spirit Possession in a Rural Area of Northern India," in W. A. Lessa and E. Z. Vogt, ed., *Reader in Comparative Religion*. Evanston: Row, Peterson.

Pfeiffer, W. M. 1971. *Transkulturelle Psychiatrie: Ergebnisse und Probleme*. Stuttgart: Georg Thieme Verlag.

Pressel, E. 1973. "Umbanda in São Paulo: Religious Innovation in a Developing Society," in Bourguignon, ed., 1973b.

Prince, Raymond, ed., 1968. *Trance and Possession States*. Montreal: R. M. Bucke Memorial Society.

Ravenscroft, K., Jr. 1962. "Spirit Possession in Haiti: A Tentative Theoretical Analysis." Unpublished bachelor's thesis, Yale University, New Haven.

Salman. D. H., O.P. 1968. "The Attitude of Catholicism toward Possession States," in Prince, ed., 1968.

Sargant, W. 1957. *Battle for the Mind*. New York: Doubleday.

Schaedel, R. P. 1966. "Introduction," in Courlander and Bastien, 1966.

Schipkowensky, N. 1963. *Der Feuertanz als magischer Brauch, als mystische Psychokatharsis und als Freudenspiel*, summarized in *Transcultural Psychiatric Research* 15:67-68 (1963).

Schreiber, F. R. 1973. *Sybil*. Chicago: Henry Regnery Co.

Spiro, M. E., ed., 1965. *Context and Meaning in Cultural Anthropology*. New York: Free Press.

Spiro, M. E. 1967. *Burmese Supernaturalism*. Englewood Cliffs, N.J.: Prentice-Hall.

Starkey, Marion 1949. *The Devil in Massachusetts*. New York: Knopf.

Starkey, Marion 1973. *The Visionary Girls*. Boston: Little, Brown.
Stevenson, Ian 1966. *Twenty Cases Suggestive of Reincarnation*. New York: American Society for Psychical Research.
Sundkler, B. 1961. *Bantu Prophets in South Africa*. London: Oxford University Press.
Thigpen, C. H., and H. M. Cleckley 1957. *The Three Faces of Eve*. New York: McGraw-Hill.
Verger, P. 1954. *Les Dieux d'Afrique*. Paris: Paul Hartmann.
Verschueren, J. 1948. *La République d'Haïti*. Wetteren, Belgium: Editions Scaldis. 3 vols.
Wallace, A. F. C. 1966. *Religion: An Anthropological View*. New York: Random House.
Weber, Max 1963. *The Sociology of Religion*. Boston: Beacon Press. (Originally published in 1922.)
Whitten, Norman E., Jr., and John F. Szwed, eds., 1970. *Afro-American Anthropology: Contemporary Perspectives*. New York: Free Press.
Williams, F. E. 1923. *The Vailala Madness*. Reprinted as Bobbs-Merrill Reprints in Anthropology, A241.
Wolf, E. R. 1955. "Types of Latin-American Peasantry: A Preliminary Discussion," *American Anthropologist* 57:452-471.
Wood, W. W. 1965. *Culture and Personality Aspects of Pentecostal Holiness Religion*. The Hague: Mouton.
Zaretsky, I. I., and M. Leone, ed. 1975. *Religious Movements in Contemporary* Evanston: Northwestern University Press.
Zaretsky, I. I., and M. Leone, ed. 1975. *Religious Movements in Contemporary America*. Princeton University Press.

SOME DOCUMENTARY FILMS SHOWING
POSSESSION TRANCE

Trance and Dance in Bali. Gregory Bateson and Margaret Mead. Filmed between 1936 and 1939; released in 1952 by New York University. 20 minutes; black and white.

Les Maîtres Fous. Jean Rouch. 1954. Possession trance rituals of the Haouka of Accra, Ghana. Braunberger, Paris; available with English narration from Mc-Graw-Hill. 25 minutes; color.

Holy Ghost People. Peter Adair. Filmed in 1966-1967 in Appalachia. Possession trance among Pentecostals. Available from Contemporary Films, New York City. 53 minutes; black and white.

The Anastenaria. P. C. Haramis and K. Kakouri. 1969. Celebration of St. Constantine's Day in Greek Macedonia by fire walking and ecstatic dancing. Available with English narration. University of California, Berkeley. 17 minutes; black and white.

INDEX

Africa:
  Haitian heritage from, 16, 28, 29
  possession belief in, 31, 35, 45, 53
  possession trance in, 31
  separatist churches in, 58-59
  societies in, 7, 34-36, 40, 46, 51, 53, 58,
    61 *also see names of societies*
  vodou influences from, 16, 18, 41
  witchcraft in, 52, 53
Afro-American peoples, 28, 29, 39, 53
Ager, Lynn, 13n
Agosto Muñoz, Nelida, 37-38
Alsace, witchcraft in, 11, 52
altered states of consciousness, 10, 64
  also see possession trance; trance—non-
    possession; hallucination
America *see* United States
American Indian societies, 10, 44-45
  also see names of societies
amoral peripheral spirit cults, 34-35, 37
Ansky, S., 65-66
Asia, possession trance in, 65

Bacon, M. K., 47
Balicki, A., 13
Barry, H., III, 47
Bastide, R., 65
Bastien, R., 32
Beattie, John, 64
Beckman, D. M., 29
Belo, Jane, 65

Blatty, W. P., 4
Boisen, A., 57
Bourguignon, E., 31, 34, 43, 48, 64
brainwashing, 60
Brazil, 18, 28, 59
Bulgaria, firewalking in, 12

Caodaism, 59
Catholicism:
  Kardecism and, 59
  vodou and, 15, 16, 55
central morality religion, 35
Charcot, J. M., 6-7
Chayefsky, Paddy, 66
Child, I. L., 47
child rearing/training, 34, 47
Christian churches, exorcism in, 3, 4, 51-52
Cleckley, H. M., 7, 38
Colson, E., 45
Courlander, H., 15, 18, 23, 32, 65
crisis cults, 61
cross-cultural studies, 10, 31, 42-43, 47
cults/cult groups, 16, 18, 30-34, 40, 50, 51
curing, 45

Dakota, Teton, 45
deprivation, as a cause of religious move-
    ments, 61
Deren, M., 15
devil worship, 55
dissociation, 7, 8, 10, 38, 40, 41

75